CLASSIC
MATCHES

PLYMOUTH ARGYLE
FOOTBALL CLUB

STADIA

CLASSIC
MATCHES

PLYMOUTH ARGYLE
FOOTBALL CLUB

JOHN LLOYD

Acknowledgements

Profits from this book will be donated to the Plymouth Argyle Supporters Training and Development Trust, a charity operated by Argyle fans which funds the youth scheme and, with Plymouth Argyle Youth Development, ensures that there is a steady supply of young players at the club.

The Argyle youth scheme has produced some great players – Martin Hodge, Gary Megson, Mike Trebilcock, Dave Phillips, Colin Sullivan, Norman Piper, Nicky Jennings, Martin Barlow, Kevin Hodges and Mickey Evans to name but a few. The current team benefits enormously from the performances of players such as Paul Wotton, Luke McCormick, Luke Summerfield, Dan Gosling and Paul Connolly. The club would be poorer without its flow of young players.

For more information on the Trust and how to help with fund-raising, please visit the website at www.argyletrust.org.uk

First published 2007

STADIA is an imprint of
Tempus Publishing Limited
The Mill, Brimscombe Port,
Stroud, Gloucestershire, GL5 2QG
www.tempus-publishing.com

© John Lloyd, 2007

British Library Cataloguing in Publication Data.
A catalogue record for this book is available from the British Library.

ISBN 978 0 7524 4149 8

Typesetting and origination by Tempus Publishing Limited.
Printed in Great Britain.

Foreword by Gordon Sparks

To be invited to write a foreword in a book is a great honour. I was asked by John to compile some notes for *Voices of Home Park* and here we are again with the second offering.

Matches are memorable for different and personal reasons. It could be for footballing genius, as displayed by Tommy Tynan when he scored four goals to defeat Blackburn Rovers, Mike Dowling with his super shot against Santos, and Paul Williams with a rare strike against Colchester United to send Plymouth Argyle to Wembley.

The bizarre may come to mind – the prime example being the abandoned game against Bradford City. It could be the unexpected – such as Hughie Reed's spectacular diving header to defeat Torquay United.

The sense of occasion is important. The night Dave Smith's side thrashed Bristol City to clinch promotion even tops Wembley for me.

Maybe your first match will be forever etched in your memory, simply because it was your first match. For me, barely old enough to attend school, it was a Saturday afternoon reserves match, but all I recall is the violent thunderstorm. I couldn't get home quickly enough!

The lows have had to be taken with the highs. For example, getting stuffed 6-1 at Highbury after the anticipation of a cup upset, despite Darran Rowbotham scoring the best goal of the game. I still contest to this day that Arsenal's fifth was offside. Changed the game, that did!

On a personal note, I would pick out the FA Cup semi-final at Villa Park, simply because it was my first commentary game on hospital radio. I only just made it in time, no thanks to the traffic congestion.

Enjoy the recollections contained on the following pages. Even if you weren't at all the games – maybe you weren't even born at the time some were played – you will no doubt relate to the sentiments of each contributor.

Being a fan of Plymouth Argyle, you know exactly that feeling of suffering and delight that has become the rollercoaster ride of following the team in green.

Here's to volume three…

Gordon Sparks
Plymouth Argyle commentator
BBC Radio Devon

Foreword by Paul Stapleton

After the great success of *Voices of Home Park*, it is a pleasure to contribute to this second book. The concept of fans telling their own stories with their own individual experiences of matches over the years has certainly made the book a must-read. I am sure there will be many memories for all of us pervading from every page.

These shared experiences last forever and the more that are in print the better. Certainly as the years go by we are all hoping for more memorable occasions to store in our memory banks, not forgetting that our younger fans are starting out on compiling their very own Argyle history.

Well, they have truly had some great occasions in the last few years with two championships. The club has progressed each year for the last five years and it is true to say that the higher up the League pyramid you get, the harder it gets each year to maintain that growth. Steady progress is the key and everyone can play their part in that.

Having been a trustee of the Plymouth Argyle Supporters Training and Development Trust from the very early days, I am well aware of the constant need for funds to maintain the excellent work being done at the Argyle Hostel and with the youth scheme. This book will help greatly with that. Well done to John Lloyd for his continued efforts and his unbridled enthusiasm.

Paul Stapleton
Chairman, Plymouth Argyle FC

Foreword by Paul Wotton

I am delighted to have been asked to add a few words of my own to this collection of heady Argyle reminiscences.

As a Plymothian who grew up watching the likes of Tommy Tynan – before going on to have the honour of playing for and captaining my hometown club – I have my own treasured memories of Home Park.

I'm also lucky enough to be able share many of the recollections that you will find in the following pages, having either watched the game in question, or been involved in it.

What this book proves is what everyone in the game knows, whether they are a director, coach or player, and that is that football is all about the fans. Anyone who says anything else simply does not understand the beautiful game.

It's interesting that not all the games in the pages that follow ended in Argyle victories, which I guess goes to show that winning is not an essential element of a memorable game – although, personally, I'd rather win a forgettable game than lose an outstanding one.

Enjoy the fifty nuggets of Pilgrims' history that follow. I'm already looking forward to the sequel.

Paul Wotton
Plymouth Argyle club captain

Introduction

When it was suggested that it might be time for a follow-up to *Voices of Home Park*, I did wonder if there would be enough interest to put another book together so soon. But when I asked for opinion from friends and from fans in the extended Argyle community, it was clear that there were dozens of new stories to be told and that another book would be welcome.

So began the process of selecting the memorable matches that you are about to read of. Argyle have played hundreds of games in League and cup since their formation in 1886 and the question of which matches should be chosen was a difficult one. The aim of this book is to give a voice to the ordinary fan for a view from the terrace, so matches from before the Second World War and even the 1950s would not be as well represented as they deserve. Perhaps other books will tell their story.

What you will find in these pages is a significant dip into Argyle's eventful history, from a thumping FA Cup win over Manchester United in 1932 through to the nerve-shredding finale to the 2003/04 Second Division Championship season and Trigger's fairytale finale at Home Park. In between are tales of glorious victories and heart-wrenching defeats, promotions and relegations, joy and despair, at home and away.

Putting a book like this together is a huge team effort and there are many people to thank for their part. Dave Rowntree has again supplied many excellent photographs, some of which have never been published before, while Mick Pengelly allowed access to his huge collection of Argyle memorabilia. Sara Raine and the team at the *Evening Herald* gave permission to raid their archives, while Keith Whitfield, Trevor Scallan at www.semperviridis.co.uk and Paul Roberts gave invaluable assistance in checking the proofs. Rick Cowdery, Steve Hill, Gordon Sparks, Paul Stapleton, Chris Errington, Alex Knee, Ian De-Lar and Rupert Metcalf all deserve a vote of thanks for their input. My grateful appreciation also goes to Holly Bennion, Rob Sharman, Lucy Chowns and the team at Tempus Publishing for their efforts, and to James Howarth for starting the ball rolling in the first place. Finally, I would like to thank my mother Lois Lloyd and her partner David Baker for their help and support.

Profits from this book will be donated to the Plymouth Argyle Supporters Training and Development Trust and, with luck, buying this book will one day help the next Mickey Evans, Paul Wotton, Paul Connolly or Luke McCormick write another chapter in Argyle's history.

John Lloyd

Classic Matches

Argyle 4	Manchester United 1	9 January 1932
Argyle 1	Wolverhampton Wanderers 1	7 January 1950
Argyle 6	Charlton Athletic 4	27 December 1960
Argyle 1	Tottenham Hotspur 5	27 January 1962
Argyle 0	Leicester City 1 (2-4 on agg)	10 February 1965
Argyle 3	Santos 2	14 March 1973
Queens Park Rangers 0	Argyle 3	20 November 1973
Argyle 1	Manchester City 1	23 January 1974
Argyle 4	Swindon Town 3	Boxing Day 1974
Blackburn Rovers 5	Argyle 2	15 February 1975
Peterborough United 1	Argyle 0	26 April 1975
Portsmouth 1	Argyle 5	21 March 1978
Argyle 3	Port Vale 2	29 April 1978
West Bromwich Albion 0	Argyle 1	18 February 1984
Derby 0	Argyle 1	14 March 1984
Watford 1	Argyle 0	14 April 1984
Argyle 4	Bristol City 0	29 April 1986
Arsenal 6	Argyle 1	31 January 1987
Portsmouth 0	Argyle 1	20 April 1987
Argyle 6	Leeds United 3	17 October 1987
Argyle 1	Everton 1	28 January 1989
Argyle 1	Arsenal 6	3 October 1989
Argyle 1	Blackburn Rovers 3	2 May 1992
Argyle 0	Exeter City 3	10 April 1993
West Bromwich Albion 2	Argyle 5	12 April 1993
Exeter City 2	Argyle 3	2 March 1994
Hartlepool United 1	Argyle 8	7 May 1994
Argyle 1	Burnley 3	18 May 1994
Argyle 1	Brentford 5	13 August 1994
Brentford 7	Argyle 0	17 December 1994
Bury 0	Argyle 5	2 September 1995

Argyle 3	Colchester United 1	15 May 1996
Argyle 1	Darlington 0	25 May 1996
Burnley 2	Argyle 1	2 May 1998
Carlisle 2	Argyle 1	8 May 1999
Cheltenham Town 2	Argyle 0	23 November 1999
Rushden & Diamonds 2	Argyle 3	27 August 2001
Exeter City 2	Argyle 3	18 September 2001
Argyle 2	Luton Town 1	29 September 2001
Argyle 3	Exeter City 0	26 February 2002
Rochdale 1	Argyle 3	26 March 2002
Carlisle 0	Argyle 2	13 April 2002
Darlington 1	Argyle 4	15 April 2002
Argyle 2	Cheltenham Town 0	20 April 2002
Port Vale 1	Argyle 5	18 October 2003
Sheffield Wednesday 1	Argyle 3	22 October 2003
Swindon Town 2	Argyle 3	13 December 2003
Argyle 7	Chesterfield 0	3 January 2004
Argyle 2	Queens Park Rangers 0	24 April 2004
Argyle 2	Ipswich Town 1	30 April 2006

ARGYLE v. MANCHESTER UNITED

Date: 9 January 1932
Location: Home Park

FA Cup third round
Attendance: 27,000

Some scoreline isn't it? Forget that it was a few years ago – all right, over seventy years ago! The fact is that it happened, and it certainly wasn't regarded on the day as a cup shock. It came shortly after a League clash between the same two teams at Home Park in which Argyle had triumphed 3-1.

And no, I wasn't at the game, but my father certainly was and he never failed to mention it to me whenever, in more recent times, Manchester United began to dominate the headlines. 'Argyle beat them you know – twice, and I'll tell you who was playing for us: Harper, Pullen…' he would say, before waxing lyrical about how one-sided the game had been. So with the passage of time, I felt as if I had actually been at the match. This was also the golden era of Sammy Black, Jack Leslie and Raymond Bowden, about whom so much has been written.

The 1931/32 season was a great campaign for Argyle, a season in which they achieved fourth place in the Second Division, scoring 100 League goals in the process. Manchester United, however, were struggling.

Not surprisingly, Argyle were favourites to go through to the next round, particularly because they had already turned over United in the League. Apparently, it was thought that the Argyle supporters felt it was a foregone conclusion and this was one explanation for the disappointing attendance of 27,000. Plymouth's last home fixture had been against fellow promotion contenders Bury, a League game that had attracted over 36,000 and saw Argyle coast home 5-1.

On Saturday 9 January 1932, the weather in Plymouth was atrocious, with driving rain and high winds. And that might just have been another factor in the poor attendance. The match went as predicted. One report said: 'Argyle's footwork continually had the United defenders struggling to turn as the ball was manoeuvred past them… the rain continued to pour and the ground became heavier, but Argyle kept up the momentum… the United goal, three minutes from time, was only a token effort… the younger fitter home side made light of the conditions.'

At the end of the game, a United director was quoted as saying he envied the home side and wished United were as good. Don't mention it to the 'Plymouth Reds'. On second thoughts, why not? And for good measure, show them the League table for the 1931/32 season.

Nigel Springthorpe

THIS SEASON SAW Argyle achieve their best ever League finish, as they came fourth in the Second Division, having scored a century of goals and won 20 of their 42 League games. Arsenal ended their FA Cup run in the fourth round, beating them 4-2 at Highbury in front of a crowd of over 65,000.

Argyle 4	Manchester United 1
Grozier (2), Vidler, Pullen	

Football Herald

VOL. 29. 1918.   REGISTERED FOR TRANSMISSION   PLYMOUTH, SATURDAY, JANUARY 9, 1932.   AS A NEWSPAPER

CUP-TIES THRILLS AND SURPRISES.

ARGYLE TO GO INTO THE HAT AGAIN

GLORIOUS WIN GAINS ENTRY TO FOURTH ROUND.

MANCHESTER UNITED SOUNDLY BEATEN AT HOME PARK.

By " PILGRIM "

HOLDERS GO OUT AFTER LEAD AT HALF-TIME.

ALL FIVE NON-LEAGUERS KNOCKED OUT

RESULTS AT A GLANCE.

Above: The *Football Herald* headline tells the story of a glorious win for Argyle.

Right: 100 goals and fourth place for the high-flying Pilgrims.

1931–32

SECOND DIVISION

		P	W	D	L	F	A	Pts
1	Wolves	42	24	8	10	115	49	56
2	Leeds	42	22	10	10	78	54	54
3	Stoke	42	19	14	9	69	48	52
4	Plymouth	42	20	9	13	100	66	49
5	Bury	42	21	7	14	70	58	49
6	Bradford PA	42	21	7	14	72	63	49
7	Bradford City	42	16	13	13	80	61	45
8	Tottenham	42	16	11	15	87	78	43
9	Millwall	42	17	9	16	61	61	43
10	Charlton	42	17	9	16	61	66	43
11	Nottm Forest	42	16	10	16	77	72	42
12	Man United	42	17	8	17	71	72	42
13	Preston	42	16	10	16	75	77	42
14	Southampton	42	17	7	18	66	77	41
15	Swansea	42	16	7	19	73	75	39
16	Notts County	42	13	12	17	75	75	38
17	Chesterfield	42	13	11	18	64	86	37
18	Oldham	42	13	10	19	62	84	36
19	Burnley	42	13	9	20	59	87	35
20	Port Vale	42	13	7	22	58	89	33
21	Barnsley	42	12	9	21	55	91	33
22	Bristol City	42	6	11	25	39	78	23

Argyle: Harper, Pullen, Roberts, Vidler, Grozier, Mackay, Titmuss, Reed, Black, Leslie, Bowden

ARGYLE v. WOLVERHAMPTON WANDERERS

Date: 7 January 1950

Location: Home Park

FA Cup third round

Attendance: 40,000

The 1949/50 season was a disaster for Plymouth Argyle. The campaign started badly and then got worse. The opening fixture was at Home Park against the dour Bradford Park Avenue, drawing a crowd of 24,767 and ending in a 1-1 draw, the away side obliging with an own goal.

Argyle then lost their next seven games and the possibility of relegation became a probability. There was a short-lived recovery in October, but then results took another nosedive. The big drop, which had just been avoided the previous season, was now on the cards. But suddenly, amidst this gloom and despair, came a break in the clouds. Argyle found themselves drawn at home in the third round of the FA Cup against the holders, Wolverhampton Wanderers.

It is difficult to convey the excitement that gripped the area. Wolves were not the Manchester United of the day – they were bigger. The England captain, Billy Wright, led a side that was laced with internationals and they were known as an attractive, attacking team.

One also has to remember that this was an age before the tacky image of players and their agents chasing the next lucrative transfer. Television sets were in the homes of only a privileged few and media coverage of our national game was to be found only in the written word. Car ownership was the exception rather than the rule, motorways and dual carriageways were still years away and consequently football supporters were limited to travel by either coach or rail.

As a result, few of those in the sell-out crowd of 40,000 that gathered at Home Park on that sunny afternoon had actually watched Wolves live. What we did know about Wolves was based solely on what we had read. Our imaginations were left to run riot. The thought of actually seeing those old gold shirts taking the field was thrilling.

At the time, the ground was open on three sides with cover at the Devonport End. My viewing position was right at the front of terracing consisting of railway sleepers, which ran the length of what is now the main Grandstand. Immediately in front, running down to the touchline, were rows of temporary seating, which had been hastily put in just for the game. I recall the public outcry that met the announcement that the price of the seats would be ten shillings. The club were accused of taking unfair advantage of their fans and had to reassure all that there would be no repeat.

Argyle's form was a revelation. It was not a case of getting stuck into the more polished opposition and attempting to rattle them. The football that they served up was quality stuff, primarily because our players were not physical types. Argyle took an early lead when Stan Williams scored at the Devonport End. A match report from one of the national papers said: 'Argyle, with their long swinging passes, quick penetration and sterling defence made the Wolves look a very ordinary combination.'

Opportunities arose to increase their lead, but were squandered. Slowly, Wolves began to assert domination, with the Argyle defence under pressure in the last fifteen minutes. Only ten minutes remained when Sammy Smyth, an Irish international, headed the Wolves equaliser. A fair result, but cup glory was

Argyle 1

Williams

Wolverhampton Wanderers 1

ARGYLE v. WOLVERHAMPTON WANDERERS

OUR PLAYERS

WILLIAM SHORTT (Goal)

TONY McSHANE (Left-half)

WILLIAM STRAUSS (Outside-right)

PADDY RATCLIFFE (Right-back)

PAT JONES (Left-back)

FRANK SQUIRES (Inside-right)

MAURICE TADMAN (Centre-forward)

NEILL DOUGALL (Right-half)

JACK CHISHOLM (Centre-half)

GEORGE DEWS (Inside-left)

STANLEY WILLIAMS (Outside-left)

Left: The Argyle squad that earned an unlikely replay at Molineux.

Below: Great excitement as Wolves come to Home Park.

so close. Argyle lost the replay at Molineux 3-0 the following Tuesday afternoon.

Then it was back to the League, with Argyle winning just three of their last seventeen games. It is interesting to note that Argyle's average attendance for the season was just over 22,000, an impressive figure by today's standards. Despite the extreme disappointment of relegation, one could take some consolation from the enduring memory of that epic cup encounter.

Nigel Springthorpe

AFTER FINISHING THE season in twenty-first position with 32 points from 42 games, Argyle were relegated to the Third Division (South). They bounced back well, ending the following year's campaign in fourth place, just missing out on promotion. The Pilgrims went back up to the Second Division as champions in 1951/52.

Who is Britain's "SPORTSMAN OF THE YEAR"?

Make sure YOUR vote is included in the Annual National Ballot organised by

SPORTING RECORD

The Family All-Sports Paper — Every week 3d.

Send your vote to: "VOTES," 184 FLEET STREET, E.C.4

GET YOUR FRIENDS TO VOTE AS WELL

JANUARY 7th, 1950 — Kick-off 2.15 p.m.

F.A. Challenge Cup, 3rd round

PLYMOUTH ARGYLE /.

versus

WOLVERHAMPTON WANDERERS /.

Official Souvenir Programme 6d.

PALE **A** ALE

The Best Bitter in the West of England

Brewed only by

THE PLYMOUTH BREWERIES LTD.

Published by Plymouth Argyle Football Co., Ltd.
Printed by Clarke, Doble & Brendon, Ltd., Oakfield Press, Plymouth

201.

Argyle: Shortt, Ratcliffe, P. Jones, Chisholm, McShane, Dews, Squires, Dougall, Tadman, Williams, Strauss.

ARGYLE v. CHARLTON ATHLETIC

Date: 27 December 1960

Location: Home Park

Football League Second Division

Attendance: 23,335

I watched this game as a twelve-year-old, with schoolmates, huddled around the concrete base of the floodlight pylon, high above the steeply sloping railway sleepers that served as terracing, in the area where the Devonport End now meets the Lyndhurst. Christmas games were usually something special.

Argyle's swaggering millionaire chairman Ron Blindell gave us a loudspeaker Christmas message about 'First Division football' being the aim. Old-timers reeked of Johnny Walker, while almost the entire crowd seemed to be smoking Wills Whiffs and wearing new overcoats from Burtons and shoes from Dolcis. Young blokes showed up in sharp Italian suits with shiny nylon ties. In those days, Argyle at home at Christmas was something you dressed up for.

To this day, Wilf Carter is my all-time Argyle hero and his performance that day remains the most accomplished I've seen from any Argyle forward. I seem to recall most of his five goals came at the Devonport End.

Four of them were typical poacher's efforts – seeing chances and seizing them with the cool of a hired assassin. The records show that he completed his hat-trick in thirty-three minutes. The fifth was from the spot. Wilf, as well as being our deadliest finisher, was also Argyle's 'penalty king'. I don't think I ever saw him miss one.

Our gang rode home to Efford, sitting upstairs in a smoke-filled, red double-decker among a busload of happy Janners. I tried playing Monopoly in the evening but couldn't concentrate. Wilf's five goals had me on an incredible high that lasted into the New Year.

I last saw Wilf at Home Park among the Parade of Legends in the Centenary season. He's an old-timer himself now, but I wish him happy Christmases for years to come. As a player, what would he be worth now?

Brian Pedley

This was a truly great game to watch. Furthermore, the result was a complete turnaround from the match played the previous day at Charlton, when the home side beat Argyle by the same margin – 6-4. The game was full of entertaining football, and of course, plenty of goals. Wilf Carter got five and Jackson scored the other. A crowd of 23,335 watched the game. I was not present at Charlton to see the away game, but Kirby scored two and Anderson and Williams got the other two.

Peter Hall

I remember the game well. At the time, Argyle were having a tough time coming off a 9-0 thrashing at Stoke. Yes – 9-0. The next game on Boxing Day was away at The Valley. Guess what? We got beaten 6-4.

With great trepidation, I decided to go to the return game with Charlton at Home Park the following day. After the last two games, I thought the attendance would be very poor. However, the crowd was over 23,000.

Argyle 6

Carter (5), Jackson

Charlton Athletic 4

Above left: An amazing game to come, with ten goals and a hat-trick.

Above right: The expected line-ups for the match – in the event there were some different names in the Argyle side.

The game was brilliant, with end-to-end attacking play from both sides. I remember three highlights of the game to this day. Argyle won 6-4. Wilf Carter – who at his best was, in my opinion, the equal of Paul Mariner – scored five goals and this is still an Argyle record.

Argyle's sixth goal was scored by Alex Jackson, which put the game out of Charlton's reach. The reaction from a large part of the crowd was amazing, as Jackson was roundly booed because he had deprived Carter of a double hat-trick. All in all, a fantastic game.

Paul Clasby

THE PILGRIMS WENT on to finish a creditable eleventh in the Second Division that season and took Aston Villa to a replay in the fourth round of the League Cup, finally going out 3-5. Argyle fans got their money's worth in this season, seeing 163 goals in 42 the Second Division games.

Argyle: McLaren, Wyatt, Stacey, J.S. Williams, Fincham, Newman, Anderson, Brown, Jackson, Carter, Maloy.

Argyle v. Tottenham Hotspur

Date: 27 January 1962

Location: Home Park

FA Cup fourth round

Attendance: 40,040

I had been dragged along to Argyle games for a few years prior to this one, but this was my first big match. My father worked for the Supporters' Club, who were Argyle's commercial arm in those days, selling rosettes, golliwogs (these were pre-PC times), handbooks and half-time draw tickets. We watched the first team ('chiefs') one week, and the reserve team ('stiffs') the next. The reserves got crowds of about 2,500 committed fans in those days.

At the very end of 1961 came my first brush with footballing fame. The reserves were playing Spurs and this was going to be the first match in their colours by the one and only Jimmy Greaves. He had gone to Milan to seek fame and fortune but it didn't work out, so Spurs signed him for the then princely sum of £99,999. As his registration was taking its time to come through, Spurs put him into their reserve team for the visit to Home Park. The media were there in droves. So were the Argyle faithful, and the not-quite-so-faithful. The attendance was nearly 13,000 – higher than even the chiefs had been getting.

That showman of an Argyle chairman, Mr Ron Blindell, made a big thing of the event and publicly welcomed a bemused young Jimmy back to England. I did likewise by shoving a specially purchased new autograph book under his nose and, graciously, the main man signed. The reserves lost 4-1, and my new mate scored two. A couple of weeks later, Argyle drew the current double holders, Spurs, in the fourth round of the FA Cup. Imagine my delight. My new hero was coming back – now where's that autograph book? 'Muuum!'

Dad and I were at the ground early. So were the Argyle faithful, not-so-faithful and, the bane of the faithful, the glory chasers. Never one to miss a trick, Mr Blindell organised a military band, the RAF police dog team and community singing. But I was focused on the main entrance.

Then it happened – the Spurs' coach arrived. Dad took time off from his duties and got me to the front of the throng surrounding the great JG. He greeted us like long-lost friends, and not only signed my book again but made sure that a number of his teammates – including the great Danny Blanchflower – did so too. Hero status was assured.

Spurs had brought the cup with them, and it was paraded around the ground on a stretcher. Just afterwards, I went around the edge of the ground with the guy selling half-time draw tickets and an older boy, Kevin Howarth, whose aunt worked for the Supporters' Club. We were awestruck by the noise and the sight of over 40,000 at Home Park, mostly standing.

We watched the game from that small building at the end of the Grandstand, which is still standing all these years later, and were amazed at how one of the best Argyle teams ever was given a lesson in how to play the game. By half-time it was 3-0 to the Spurs – goals by Terry Medwin, Cliff Jones and, yes, Jimmy, my main man. It should have been more, though Argyle had their moments too.

But the best was yet to come – first, a goal by my hero that would have put Maradona at his best to shame. A jink to the left, a jink to the right and then the trademark Greaves precision finish. Poor Dave McLaren, one of the best Argyle goalies ever, had no chance.

Argyle 1

Anderson

Tottenham Hotspur 5

THE FOOTBALL ASSOCIATION CHALLENGE CUP COMPETITION

Fourth Round Tie

PLYMOUTH ARGYLE *1.*

versus

TOTTENHAM HOTSPUR *5.*

SATURDAY, JANUARY 27th, 1962

Kick-off 3 p.m.

Home Park   Plymouth

Souvenir Programme - One Shilling

Jimmy Greaves and the double holders come to Home Park.

PLYMOUTH ARGYLE *1.* (Green and Black Shirts, White Shorts)

Goal
DAVE McLAREN

2 *Right Back*
GEORGE ROBERTSON

3 *Left Back*
BRYCE FULTON

4 *Right Half*
JOHNNY WILLIAMS

5 *Centre Half*
GORDON FINCHAM

6 *Left Half*
JOHNNY NEWMAN

8 *Inside Right*
WILF CARTER

10 *Inside Left*
JIMMY McANEARNEY

7 *Outside Right*
PETER ANDERSON

9 *Centre Forward*
GEORGE KIRBY

11 *Outside Left*
KEN MALOY

Referee:
R. E. SMITH
(*Newport*)

MILLBAY
CLEANERS of CLOTHES
Have No Match!

Linesmen:
W. F. J. SUMMERHAYES
(Bristol)   Red Flag
H. V. GISBORNE (*Sherborne*)
Amber Flag

11 *Outside Left*
C. JONES *.*

10 *Inside Left*
J. GREAVES *. J.*

9 *Centre Forward*
L. ALLEN

8 *Inside Right*
WHITE

7 *Outside Right*
T. MEDWIN

6 *Left Half*
D. MACKAY

5 *Centre Half*
M. NORMAN

4 *Right Half*
D. BLANCHFLOWER

3 *Left Back*
R. HENRY

2 *Right Back*
P. BAKER

W. BROWN
Goal

(White Shirts, Blue Shorts)   **TOTTENHAM HOTSPUR** *5.*

ANY CHANGES IN THE ABOVE TEAMS WILL BE ANNOUNCED

TIME TABLE AND PROGRAMME OF EVENTS

1.30 p.m. to 2.15 p.m.	**The Band of the Devonshire and Dorset Regiment** (by kind permission of the Commanding Officer Lieutenant Colonel P. T. Willcocks, M.C., M.B.E.). **Bandmaster:** Mr. K. R. R. Boulding, L.R.A.M., A.R.C.M., B.B.C.M.	2.30 p.m. to 2.50 p.m. — **Community Singing** (arranged by the *Daily Express*). Conductor: **Arthur Caiger, D.C.M.** Accompanied by the Band.
		3.0 p.m. — Kick-off.
		3.45 p.m. — Half-Time. **Music by the Band.**
2.15 p.m. to 2.30 p.m.	**Display by The Royal Air Force Police Dog Demonstration Team**	4.40 p.m. — End of Match.

H. 1.
0-3.

The fan who bought this programme seems to have been more interested in the Spurs' goalscorers than Anderson, who scored Argyle's consolation goal.

Not long after, Argyle got one back, by right-winger Peter Anderson – the unsung hero of the Argyle team that almost made it to the top division. But just to make the point, Spurs completed the scoring through the sublime John White, later to be tragically struck down by lightning.

A great game, a great occasion – pity about the result. Not that most fans went home unhappy. Mr Blindell was certainly pleased, but not as much as I was. I have never met the great JG since that day, but I have followed his career with intense interest. Jimmy apart, probably no one was more disappointed than me when that nasty Alf Ramsey left him out of the World Cup final team. No one was more upset to see him go off the rails thereafter. It's good to see that he has come through it a bigger and better man. Now, if only Argyle Youth Development could unearth the next Jimmy Greaves.

Kevin Howarth and I continued to follow Argyle through all of their tribulations and the occasional triumph, but lost touch when we left school. Then, over forty years after the Spurs match, at an unimportant, end-of-season game at Swindon, John Lloyd introduced me to one of the *Voices of Home Park* publishing team, James Howarth. Suddenly his father, sitting next to him, repeated my name – he's the Kevin of the great walk-around. Then we were no longer at the dreary County Ground in 2003, but back at the Theatre of Greens in January 1962.

The next time I went to the Swindon County Ground, my son Matthew's name came out of the Junior Greens' hat to be the Argyle mascot. That tactical maestro, Mr Paul Sturrock, invited us into the changing room to meet the team, and Matty was surrounded by his heroes – the great David, Cocko, Stevie Adams, Trigger and Wottsie – who all greeted him as enthusiastically as JG had greeted me.

So the cycle goes on and, on that dull, dreary, damp day in the land of the Magic Roundabout, the lads did not muck it up!

Keith Whitfield

IN AN EXCELLENT season for the Greens, the team went on to finish in fifth place in the Second Division, having picked up wins against Southampton, Leeds United, Newcastle United and Sunderland amongst others.

Argyle: McLaren, Robertson, Fulton, J.S. Williams, Fincham, Newman, Anderson, Carter, Kirby, McAnearney, Maloy.

Argyle v. Leicester City

Date: 10 February 1965

Location: Home Park

League Cup semi-final (second leg)

Attendance: 20,780

Argyle were on the edge of the final of a major cup competition at Wembley and I was allowed to stay up late and go to the match. All that the Pilgrims had to do was beat Leicester City – who were in the First Division and were the League Cup holders – by two goals on our own turf. OK, they had the England goalie, Gordon Banks, there to stop us, but we were ready for anything.

Our new manager, Malcolm Allison (Big Mal) had fired everyone up. He had surprised our lofty opponents in the first leg at Filbert Street by encouraging our depleted team to have a go at them. Reserve-team players, including the youthful Richard Reynolds and Norman Piper, were given starts and they gave it everything. Argyle narrowly lost 3-2 after a disputed goal in the last few minutes, but they knew that they could match their illustrious opponents in the return leg.

Over 20,000 turned up on a cold February night to roar on Big Mal's boys (dwarfing the 12,000 that had attended the first leg). They were cheered by the news that Barrie Jones (our most expensive player), Nicky Jennings, Cliff Jackson and, surprisingly, Frank Lord were fit to play. So out went Reynolds, Piper and the irrepressible Dave 'Sooty' Corbett.

Our team was Dwyer, Book, Reeves, Neale, Newman, Williams, Jones, Trebilcock, Lord, Jackson and Jennings. Tony Book (who had recently entered professional football in his late twenties) was to follow Big Mal to Manchester City and make a name for himself there. Mike Trebilcock went to Everton and scored two goals to give them an unlikely win in the 1966 FA Cup final.

My hero was Johnny S. Williams, said to be the target of a number of First Division clubs, who had the hardest shot I had ever seen. Dad said that only the late and great Duncan Edwards could strike a ball better than Johnny, often waxing lyrical about the day at Wembley when he saw the big guy hit a screamer against the Scots.

The Home Park crowd gave it everything for the boys with the green hoop, but it never really looked as if they would score. Frank Lord was completely out of sorts – hardly surprising for someone just returning after a broken leg – and Jones and Jennings had little room to work in.

Ten minutes before half-time, Leicester's John Sjoberg hammered home a short corner, and Argyle had a mountain to climb. Johnny Williams tried his best, but the Banks of England was more than equal to his efforts. Big Mal ranted and raved up and down the touchline in his Cossack hat, much to the annoyance of the officials, but it looked less and less like our night.

With ten minutes to go, Dad said, 'Right, you've got school tomorrow' and we were off to the car park for the journey home (and there was I hoping for extra time and an even later night).

So we didn't get to Wembley that time, nor the next two times (the League Cup semi-final in 1974 and the play-offs in 1994), but we did get there in 1996 and, despite the fact that it was the basement play-off, I was proud to be there supporting the Pilgrims with my Dad, talking of such things as what might have

Argyle 0

Leicester City 1 (2-4 on aggregate)

Above: The 'smart' challengers line up in the first leg against the Foxes.

Right: The programme from the first game at Filbert Street.

OFFICIAL PROGRAMME
6^D.

LEICESTER CITY FOOTBALL CLUB

SEASON
1964
1965

F.A. CUP 4th ROUND
LEICESTER CITY
v
PLYMOUTH ARGYLE
SATURDAY 30th JANUARY 1965

been had Big Mal played Reynolds instead of Lord, and had Stringfellow been pulled up for handball in the first leg.

Keith Whitfield

THE LEAGUE CUP run took its toll on Argyle's League form and they finished fifteenth in the Second Division that season, playing in front of an average Home Park crowd of 14,649.

Argyle: Dwyer, Book, Newman, Reeves, Neale, Jones, Jackson, Trebilcock, Williams, Lord, Jennings.

Argyle v. Santos

Date: 14 March 1973

Location: Home Park

Friendly

Attendance: 37,639

I was in my last year at school in Truro when this game came along and I can still recall many things about that remarkable evening. Several school friends met me at Truro station to catch the football special that had been laid on. The train was already full when we got on and this was the first indication of the interest the game had generated.

The previous World Cup was still fresh in our minds and the chance to see the great Pele and Carlos Alberto had brought people out in their droves. Every station had more people trying to pack onto the train, which even stopped at places like Menheniot and St Germans. Having totally underestimated the interest, the train schedule did not allow much time to get to the game.

We rushed up the hill from the station and joined some of the queues for the Mayflower terrace. We managed to get in before kick-off and found everyone packed at the back, obviously unused to being in a big crowd and having to push their way through. We were just about able to see most of the pitch, standing on tiptoes, and witnessed the teams coming out. Like the rest of the crowd, we were completely unaware of the wrangling going on in the changing rooms and the handing over of large wads of cash to get the players out there.

Santos played the game at a stroll and a swagger, whilst Argyle played it like a cup final. When the first goal went in, there was a reaction of surprise and we thought they were happy to let us have a goal. The opening goal came only minutes into the game, from Cornishman Mike Dowling who let fly from distance.

This amazing strike was one that could have disappeared into the Zoo, but it stopped in the top corner of the net. Mike Dowling never made it at Plymouth and later went on to play rugby for Bodmin Second XV, but he had joined the Argyle legends with this goal. When the second goal went in from Rickard, the attitude of the Brazilians suddenly changed, the great Carlos Alberto remonstrated at length with the referee, claiming it was offside, which it probably was.

The goal stood and Santos, who had strolled around not looking too interested, now showed that they didn't intend losing to Plymouth. However, things were to get worse for the Brazilians as Hinch made it 3-0 from close range before half-time.

In the second half, Edu – a new name to us – came to the fore, running straight through our defence almost at will. We thought he would go on to great things, but he never really hit the heights for his country. Following the few customary changes of friendly matches, on came Melia Aleksic for his Argyle debut, taking over from Jim Furnell. The Argyle defence finally cracked as the Brazilians showed they were also adept at going down in the box and the referee didn't need much persuading to give a penalty. Maybe he had also received an ultimatum from the Brazilians before kick-off.

Seeing Pele score was probably the main objective of everyone in the 38,000 crowd packed into Home Park that March evening. They got their reward as Pele knocked the penalty past Aleksic, who got his first touch for Argyle picking it out of the net.

Argyle 3

Dowling, Rickard, Hinch

Santos 2

The identity of the main attraction is no surprise as Santos come to Plymouth.

Pele had not been as outstanding as we expected but was soon involved again, putting Edu in for an easy second to set up a tense finish. Amazingly, Argyle held on for the 3-2 win, which was definitely not in the Santos script and Carlos Alberto maintained the second goal was offside many years later in a TV flashback programme.

My recollections of the rest of the evening are not as clear. We had to rush back down the hill for the return of the badly-timed football special. To have seen one of the world's greatest ever footballers score at Home Park was the best recollection from the evening, along with the Mike Dowling special.

Chris Dennis

THE SANTOS GAME was a highlight in one of those seasons when Argyle neither threatened promotion nor flirted with relegation. They eventually finished eighth in the Third Division with an average attendance of just over 9,000.

Argyle: Furnell (Aleksic), Provan, Sullivan, Hore, Saxton, Hague, Dowling, Rickard, Hinch (Davey), Latcham, Welsh.

QUEENS PARK RANGERS v. ARGYLE

Date: 20 November 1973
Location: Loftus Road

Football League Cup fourth round
Attendance: 19,072

Some games stick in the memory as being more than simply great wins in their own right. This match was special not only for being a great victory, but also because it represented a crucial stage in the emergence of Waiters' Wonders – a team that won promotion in an exciting fashion the following season, and which contained a future England star.

Argyle had been having a poor season. The new young manager, Tony Waiters, had pulled together a decent looking team, but one that couldn't seem to put in consistently good performances. Waiters had replaced the legend that was Jimmy Hinch with a lad plucked from Chorley Town called Paul Mariner. You can imagine the fun that the press had with the Pilgrims signing a Mariner. Oh, how we laughed – not!

The League Cup offered some kind of solace from League frustration. Argyle had beaten Torquay, our traditional rivals, Portsmouth, and Waiters' ex-club Burnley on the way to this plum tie away to QPR.

At the time, they were the highest placed London club, and unfurled a flag just before the match to announce this to the world. Their team was composed of well-known players, most on their way down from glittering careers (including Terry Venables, Frank McLintock and Terry Mancini), with some travelling in the opposite direction (such as Phil Parkes, Gerry Francis and Stan Bowles). For most of their fans, this match was a formality on the way to further League Cup glory – but nobody told that to the men in green and black stripes.

From the first whistle, Argyle took the game to the big shots from the big city. That lump of Cornish granite on legs – as Waiters termed John Hore – and the classy Ernie Machin took control of midfield. Mariner and Stephen Davey were giving the not-so-young legs of McLintock and Mancini the run-around. The two Alans – Rogers and Welsh – were feeding the front two a steady supply of ammunition.

Argyle looked like the home team and Rangers were reduced to the occasional counter-attack. Only Parkes' renowned shot-stopping abilities prevented a hatful of Argyle goals. The Greens should have been well in front by half-time, but the first half ended 0-0.

The second half started in the same way and it was no surprise when the Greens went in front. Welsh, who had been tormenting the ageing QPR defence all match, bamboozled McLintock and squeezed the ball between Parkes and the post.

Rather than simply defend their advantage, Argyle went looking for more. They were rewarded when Mariner used his strength to win the ball in the penalty area, and Davey gave his precise pass its just desserts, to double Argyle's advantage.

QPR responded by bringing on a blonde-haired midfielder called John Delve. However, his main task was picking the ball out of the net as Welsh scored his second and Argyle's third, prompting the Argyle faithful to sing 'easy, easy, easy' as the QPR fans left in droves.

Delve must have impressed Waiters, though, as he was the one chosen to replace skipper Machin at the centre of Argyle's midfield when the General left at the end of the season.

Queens Park Rangers 0

Argyle 3
Welsh (2), Davey

QUEENS PARK RANGERS *v.* ARGYLE

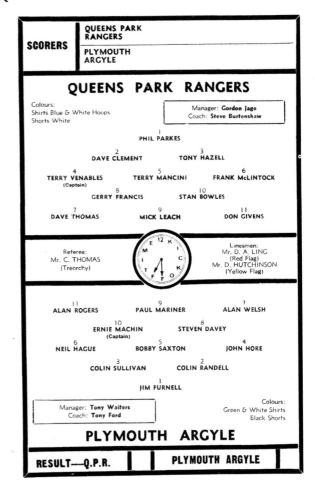

SCORERS	QUEENS PARK RANGERS
	PLYMOUTH ARGYLE

QUEENS PARK RANGERS

Colours:
Shirts Blue & White Hoops
Shorts White

Manager: **Gordon Jago**
Coach: **Steve Burtenshaw**

1
PHIL PARKES

2
DAVE CLEMENT

3
TONY HAZELL

4
TERRY VENABLES
(Captain)

5
TERRY MANCINI

6
FRANK McLINTOCK

8
GERRY FRANCIS

10
STAN BOWLES

7
DAVE THOMAS

9
MICK LEACH

11
DON GIVENS

Referee:
Mr. C. THOMAS
(Treorchy)

Linesmen:
Mr. D. A. LING
(Red Flag)
Mr. D. HUTCHINSON
(Yellow Flag)

11
ALAN ROGERS

9
PAUL MARINER

7
ALAN WELSH

10
ERNIE MACHIN
(Captain)

8
STEVEN DAVEY

6
NEIL HAGUE

5
BOBBY SAXTON

4
JOHN HORE

3
COLIN SULLIVAN

2
COLIN RANDELL

1
JIM FURNELL

Manager: **Tony Waiters**
Coach: **Tony Ford**

Colours:
Green & White Shirts
Black Shorts

PLYMOUTH ARGYLE

| RESULT—Q.P.R. | | PLYMOUTH ARGYLE | |

Famous names for QPR, but the heavily fancied London side are undone by Argyle.

Argyle went back to League action in a buoyant mood, but the inconsistent form continued. They did get to the semi-finals of the League Cup, beating Birmingham 2-1 at St Andrew's on the way, with goals by Davey and Welsh. That was the third First Division scalp on the trot. The semi-final loss to Manchester City ended this dream run. Unusually, these later matches were played in mid-week daytime, during the three-day-week power crisis of the time.

For Argyle fans, the QPR tie was the match when hopes of a brave new dawn for the boys in green started to carry some weight, and when Waiters began to see how he could harness the qualities of the team that he had inherited with his own vision of how the beautiful game should be played.

Keith Whitfield

Argyle: Furnell, Randell, Sullivan, Hore, Hague, Saxton, Johnson, Davey, Mariner, Machin, Rogers.

ARGYLE v. MANCHESTER CITY

Date: 23 January 1974
Location: Home Park

League Cup semi-final (first leg)
Attendance: 30,390

I was a schoolboy at the time of the game. I had a proud record of not having missed an Argyle home game for three years and, needless to say, wasted no time in buying my ticket to the match. My parents kindly agreed to write me a sick note to explain my absence from school. I was going to be at Home Park come what may. The fact that it was to be played during school time was of minor relevance. Unfortunately, matters took some an unexpected course.

Firstly, the school threatened to suspend any pupil who took unauthorised leave. To my young mind that almost seemed like an incentive. But then, as if that wasn't bad enough, they organised an official school outing to the game, which was marshalled by the most draconian teachers they could find, who were also instructed to look out for any 'unofficial' attendees. Consequently, I spent significant parts of the game looking over my shoulder to evade capture. It didn't help that the highlights (including crowd shots) were shown later on local TV, but I think I got away with it.

Watching the highlights on the Centenary DVD, I actually think I caught sight of myself with regulation parka coat and scarf tied round my wrist in my usual spot at the front of the terraces – scary stuff. Just hope I don't get summoned back for detention some thirty-odd years on.

Roger Ball

I remember two things about this game. Firstly, it had a bizarre afternoon mid-week kick-off time because of power restrictions being in place, due to the Ted Heath era three-day week. Hyde Park Juniors profited hugely, because everybody got the afternoon off!

Secondly, I recall Mike Summerbee picking up the toilet roll that had streamed onto the pitch near the touchline in front of the Grandstand. Then they passed the ball to him and he was rolling up the toilet roll as he ran down the wing.

Roger Willis

I recall that, as a schoolboy, we were allowed the afternoon off to go to the game. The pitch was covered in puddles due to torrential rain – the game would probably not have been played in the modern era. The pitch was little more than a quagmire and passes got stuck in the water throughout the game.

Steve Davey scored for Argyle and, with 30,000 in the ground, hopes for another famous League Cup win were raised, but City had a class team including Marsh, Lee, Bell and Summerbee and scored an equaliser from a corner at the Devonport End. The second leg at Maine Road resulted in a 2-0 defeat for Argyle.

Adrian Jones

Argyle 1
  Davey

Manchester City 1

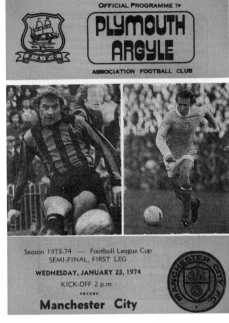

Above: Argyle's Ernie Machin and City's Mike Summerbee feature on the cover of the programme.

Above, left: Argyle take on Manchester City.

Below, left: A fine performance earned a replay at Maine Road.

THE EMBRYONIC 'Waiters' Wonders' finished in seventeenth place in the Third Division, in front of an average crowd of less than 8,000. The following season, crowds would double as the Pilgrims challenged for promotion.

Argyle: Furnell, Randell, Sullivan, Hore, Hague, Saxton, Johnson, Davey, Mariner, Machin, Rogers.

ARGYLE v. SWINDON TOWN

Date: Boxing Day 1974,
Location: Home Park

Football League Third Division
Attendance: 18,027

Every season has pivotal matches that determine whether it is one to remember or one to forget. The 1974/75 promotion season had more than its fair share, but the pivotal match was the Christmas cracker against Swindon Town. It gave the team the confidence that they could more than match the best in the Division.

The season did not start well – 6 losses in the first 10 games. By the time I had returned to college in early October, it looked like another season of trying to avoid the drop to the basement division. And it got worse. At this time, Argyle and Port Vale were locked in warfare that had culminated in the infamous Black Sunday (10 March 1974), when three Argyle players got their marching orders (Steve Davey, Bobby Saxton and Dave Provan) and Paul Mariner broke his nose. This time around it was less brutal, but a 2-0 loss put Argyle well off the pace.

The main thing going for the team at this time was the burgeoning partnership between Mariner and his new brother-at-arms, Billy Rafferty. To support them, manager Tony Waiters changed the team about. On the right side of midfield, he brought in a blond-haired youngster called Brian Johnson; for the left side of midfield, he cunningly acquired Hughie McAuley from Liverpool.

Now the dynamic duo had players who could not only give them the service they deserved but also contribute to the goal-scoring as well. McAuley was an instant fans' favourite; Johnson had his doubters, but never the manager.

After the Port Vale defeat, 'Waiters' Wonders' went on a winning run, moving up to ninth place at Christmas. Doubts still lingered, though, about their ability to mix it with the best in the league. A crucial test was the Boxing Day match against third-placed Swindon.

It started badly. After twenty minutes, Dave Moss put the Robins ahead, and doubled the advantage after half an hour. For a moment there was silence, but then the big festive crowd got right behind the team. Gradually, the steely midfield combination of John Delve and Colin Randell took control. A free-kick on the edge of the box just before half-time gave Randell his chance, and the no-nonsense Welshman curled the ball around the wall and into the goal.

Straight after the break, the Greens gave it everything and Delve headed us level before many had returned to their places. Swindon immediately restored their advantage, but the ever-threatening Mariner pulled it back level midway through the second half.

With less than a quarter of an hour to go, Argyle were awarded a penalty. The previous Saturday, Terry Venables had had a penalty saved by the Argyle goalie, Jim Furnell – 'Come on without, Come on within, You'll not see nothin' like the mighty Jim' – in the last minute of the FA Cup match, to give Argyle victory over Malcolm Allison's all-star Crystal Palace team. The roar could be heard by the Christmas shoppers in Royal Parade. On this occasion, a similar roar greeted the scoring of Argyle's winner by the cool Rafferty – 'Oooh, Billy, Billy; Billy, Billy, Billy, Billy Raff-erty'.

Argyle 4
Randell, Delve, Mariner, Rafferty

Swindon Town 3

A decisive game as Argyle beat the Robins in a Home Park thriller.

After this match, Argyle quickly climbed the table, thumping Bournemouth 7-3 at their place and beating the League leaders Blackburn 2-1 at Home Park on the way. By mid-April, they were top and were promoted.

A disappointing home draw against Port Vale, when the referee disallowed a solo Rafferty goal on the grounds that Mariner was standing offside, and a last-match loss at Peterborough handed the championship to Blackburn by one point. But the feel-good factor had returned to Home Park.

It didn't last long. After two seasons in the Second Division, the sale of Rafferty and Mariner and the failure of their replacements to perform led to relegation and the resignation of Waiters. There ensued almost a decade of constant flirting with relegation. Mariner went to Bobby Robson's Ipswich and, before long, he became England's no.9. Of course, he wasn't the first mariner from Plymouth to lead the line for his country. But the other bloke favoured a different round-ball game.

Keith Whitfield

Argyle: Furnell, Hore, Delve, Mariner, McAuley, Green, Burrows P, Saxton, Rafferty, Johnson, Randell. Sub: Rogers.

BLACKBURN ROVERS v. ARGYLE

Date: 15 February 1975

Location: Ewood Park

Football League Third Division

Attendance: 17,734

It was first against second and we had beaten them 2-1 at home eleven days earlier. My memories of this game start on the previous evening.

Friday evening, 14 February

I was one of a group of sixteen-year-olds from Southway Comprehensive School who planned to go to the game and were travelling up on the official club coaches, leaving from Home Park at 1a.m. Most of the other coaches were leaving at either 11p.m. or midnight.

As we had hours to kill prior to getting on the coaches, we decided to meet up at the SWEB social club where we knew we would get served. After a few pints and having been kicked out at closing time, we were at a loss as to what we could do to kill the couple of hours remaining until the coaches left. We decided to go into the town centre.

As we walked (swayed) down New George Street, one of the group noticed the large Green and White House of Fraser flag hanging off the flagpole on the side of the Dingles building. In our lager-induced state, we immediately started having bets about who could climb up and get the flag. I ended up with the short straw. Fortunately, the block walls of the Dingles building are akin to steps and, by using these to climb the first fifteen feet or so, I made it to the base of the flagpole and then shinned up the pole to release the flag.

Saturday 15 February

After walking through Central Park, we started to pick the white writing and stags head off the flag until the coaches arrived, and by the time we got to Blackburn, the flag was plain green.

Blackburn, 7a.m.

We arrived in Blackburn at 7a.m. and we were dropped off near to the town centre. We could not believe our eyes – there were in excess of 4,000 Argyle fans already in the town and there was an expectation that another two full football special trains were arriving mid-morning, but the most amazing thing was that just about everything as far as the eye could see had been sprayed green, white and black.

Walls, shops, cars, houses, street signs – even a local road sweeper had had one side of his face sprayed green. It was absolute chaos. Shops were being ransacked and a serious amount of vandalism had taken place. We decided that discretion was probably the best part of valour, and found an area away from the main town where we could await the game in safety.

The ground, at about 2.20p.m.

What do I remember about the ground? Well, it was the first ground I had been to where the refreshment stand at the back of the away end was open all through the game, and also the first that served alcohol

Blackburn Rovers 5	Argyle 2
	McAuley, o.g.

during the game as well. We were more drunk when we came out after the game than when we had gone in.

The game, first half, 3p.m.

The game started well for us and within the first fifteen minutes we had had a couple of chances. Then came the breakthrough. Hugh McAuley scored, we were one up and the sound in the enclosed away end was amazing. About fifteen minutes later, it got even better when, after a prolonged spell of pressure, one of the Blackburn players put the ball through his own net.

Life didn't get much better than that, or so we thought, but for the next ten minutes Blackburn were all over us and just before the half-time break, the inevitable happened. John Delve gave away a penalty, we were gutted, but without reason as Jim Furnell saved the spot-kick and two minutes later the half-time whistle went. We couldn't believe our luck.

Above: The Pilgrims score first, but it is not to be.

Right: Programme from the day Blackburn became 'Greenburn'.

The second half, 4p.m.

Well, what can I say about the second half? I have tried to wipe most of it from my mind. Blackburn came straight out of the blocks at us, and it was not long before they had pulled one goal back, it seemed like even less time before they were level, and I am afraid things just went quickly downhill from there. The final score was 5-2. Blackburn stayed top and we were gutted. The trip home that day has to be one of the longest I have had – to be so exhilarated by half-time and then to reach the depths of despair within an hour took its toll.

The aftermath

The amount of damage and destruction caused by Argyle fans that day was vast, and the mayor of Blackburn went on record to say that his town had been changed to 'Greenburn' for the day. He said how amazed they were by the number of people that had turned up to support Argyle, although they were disappointed with the behaviour of some of the Argyle fans. This was partly due to a lack of policing, as they were not expecting in excess of 6,000 away fans.

The flag

Well, the flag was one of the first large Argyle flags to be taken regularly around the country. It had a black upright cross and a white diagonal cross sewn onto it in the manner of a green, black and white Union Jack, and was seen at Argyle's home and away matches for many years, but I do not know what finally happened to it.

Eddie Bray

Argyle: Furnell, Hore, Delve, Mariner, McAuley, Green, P. Burrows, Saxton, Rafferty, Johnson, Randell.

Peterborough United v. Argyle

Date: 26 April 1975   Football League Third Division
Location: London Road   Attendance: 11,176

It was the last game of the season, Argyle were top and a win would give us the title.

I was once again among a group of sixteen-year-olds from Southway Comp who had arranged to go on the Argyle official coaches leaving from Home Park at 4a.m. Due to the previous problems at Blackburn – and a couple of other venues during the season – the police had insisted that the coaches left Plymouth later and thus arrived closer to the start time of the game. It was a good thing that they did, as over 9,000 Argyle fans made the trip up to Peterborough.

We decided to visit our usual haunt on the Friday night and after closing time managed to blag our way into a nightclub to pass more time until the coaches left. When we arrived at Home Park car park, one of our number turned up with a couple of bags of ale for the journey.

Just prior to this, the government had passed a law that no alcohol was to be consumed on football coaches, so we had to laugh when, as we boarded the coach, the steward (yes, we even had them in those days) asked us if we had any alcohol with us. After saying no, the bottles were clinking as we walked down the aisle of the coach.

We arrived in Peterborough at about midday and walked around the town, getting searched about every 400 yards and as I was wearing the large flag (previously procured) like a cape, I seemed to be singled out for special attention. By about 1.30p.m., we had had enough of the town and made our way towards the ground. By this time, there must have been 4,000 or 5,000 waiting outside the gates, which the officials told us they would not be opening until 2.30p.m.

As you can imagine, this went down like a lead balloon with the Argyle supporters and, with a concerted push, they pushed the main gates down and made their way into the ground. We thought we had saved our gate money as the police allowed us to stay in the ground (where they could control us) and I can remember an Argyle fan setting fire to a blue and white scarf on the centre spot during this time.

Our enjoyment at getting in free was to be short-lived as, at about 2 p.m., there was an announcement saying that if we did not vacate the ground and queue in a reasonable manner, the game would be postponed. This we all did, eventually.

The match was a pretty nervy affair with a s—— referee (have I said we always get s—— refs?) and after having a stonewall penalty claim ignored, we went on to lose the game 1-0. Blackburn Rovers having won meant we finished in second place behind them.

At the end of the game, there was a massive pitch invasion and pretty much everyone ran across the pitch and jumped over the wall into the Peterborough end. As I have said, there were in excess of 9,000 Argyle fans and the total gate was only 11,100. I would imagine the number of Peterborough fans in their end was less than 1,000 and there was utter carnage.

On the way back to the coach, all I could see was devastation again. There was a new block of flats that had just been built and I could not see one window that had not been smashed. Below this, a policeman

---

Peterborough United 1   Argyle 0

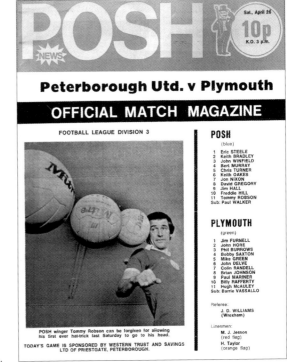

Peterborough Utd. v Plymouth

OFFICIAL MATCH MAGAZINE

FOOTBALL LEAGUE DIVISION 3

POSH
(blue)

1 Eric STEELE
2 Keith BRADLEY
3 John WINFIELD
4 Bert MURRAY
5 Chris TURNER
6 Keith OAKES
7 Jon NIXON
8 David GREGORY
9 Jim HALL
10 Freddie HILL
11 Tommy ROBSON
Sub: Paul WALKER

PLYMOUTH
(green)

1 Jim FURNELL
2 John HORE
3 Phil BURROWS
4 Bobby SAXTON
5 Mike GREEN
6 John DELVE
7 Colin RANDELL
8 Brian JOHNSON
9 Paul MARINER
10 Billy RAFFERTY
11 Hugh McAULEY
Sub: Barrie VASSALLO

Referee:
J. D. WILLIAMS
(Wrexham)

Linesmen:
M. J. Jesson
(red flag)
H. Taylor
(orange flag)

POSH winger Tommy Robson can be forgiven for allowing his first ever hat-trick last Saturday to go to his head.

TODAY'S GAME IS SPONSORED BY WESTERN TRUST AND SAVINGS LTD OF PRIESTGATE, PETERBOROUGH.

So close to a title, but the Pilgrims won promotion to the Second Division nonetheless.

had managed to get himself cut off and was being stoned. There was a tremendous amount of damage inflicted on that town and I could not believe some of the scenes that I was seeing. My only thought at the time was, 'thank God I'm dressed in green and talk with a South-West accent'.

This season was a golden age for football at Plymouth Argyle and the team played some remarkably good stuff. We had a world class pair of strikers and, whilst Paul Mariner went on to better things, he had a fantastic partnership with Billy Rafferty.

Tony Waiters was a superb manager and if he hadn't fallen out with Robert Daniels, who knows where he could have taken Argyle.

But, on the other hand, it was one of the worst times for football hooliganism. Whilst the hooligans were only at the 'give the opposition a kicking' stage, it would not be long before a much more sinister aspect would creep into the picture.

Plymouth Argyle fans of the 1974/75 season had a reputation for hooliganism, not necessarily for being harder than other clubs' fans (Chelsea, West Ham and Manchester United had that dubious honour) but for the vast numbers they took to away matches and the devastation they left behind.

Eddie Bray

Argyle: Furnell, Hore, Johnson, Mariner, McAuley, Green, P. Burrows, Saxton, Rafferty, Delve, Randell. Sub: Vassallo.

PORTSMOUTH v. ARGYLE

Date: 21 March 1978

Location: Fratton Park

Football League Third Division

Attendance: 11,010

My father was in the Royal Navy and we moved to Gosport late in 1977. Being new to the area and having only just started my first job, I didn't have anyone to go to the match with.

I remember doubting whether I should go as it was a bit tricky for a spotty youth without transport. A bus, ferry, train and a walk would be required to get there. In the end, I decided I just couldn't pass up the opportunity.

Now, how I managed to get into the home terracing in front of the main stand I'll never know. With my scarf remaining safe in my pocket, I tried to watch the game without showing any emotion as the home fans were getting a little annoyed at the way Argyle dominated the match.

My first away game and Argyle were thrashing their port rivals, and I couldn't cheer any of the goals. The match itself was a blur to be honest as the locals were fighting among themselves and I was more concerned with my own safety than the match. I do remember that there were not many Argyle fans there that night to witness a great spectacle.

After the game, I was trying to hide my delight on the walk back to the station. Once on the train and sitting reading the match programme, I thought my evening was about to be ruined when two little fourteen or fifteen-year-old thugs came into my carriage, resplendent with scarves and Doc Martens. After attempting to kick everything from doors to seats, they sat opposite me (the rest of the carriage was empty) and started moaning about how bad we (Pompey) were and that someone was going to pay. They then asked me where my scarf was! I told them that a group of Argyle fans had jumped me and pinched it.

This saved me, though they did point out that I didn't look too unhappy and couldn't be a true fan. With their mood not improved, they proceeded to restart their destruction of the carriage.

At one point, as they were trying to kick the bulbs in the ceiling by swinging on the luggage racks, a ticket inspector came in, saw what they were doing and did an about turn. Cheers for that! Fortunately, Portsmouth Harbour station saved me, and the carriage, from further abuse. A very strange evening for this spotty seventeen-year-old Green.

Stuart Bloye

Cold – that's what I remember more than anything else. Mum suffered at that time from bad circulation and had bought some sort of patented hand warmer from the back pages of the *Sunday Express*. She swears it saved her fingers that night, but I reckon she simply wasn't clapping enough.

That was the problem. My family are from Portsmouth, so we had to stand with them on the Popular side. Of course, you had to be extra careful in those days, but I remember that when the fifth went in, three brave Argyle fans joyously invaded the pitch from the Milton End. They were escorted away via the (home) Fratton End to a colourful reception. Rather them than me.

Portsmouth 1	Argyle 5
	Trusson, Binney (2), Taylor, Fear

Above: The Pompey chimes are silenced by a rampant Argyle team.

Right: An impressive win for Argyle against their traditional port rivals.

POMPEY
THE OFFICIAL PROGRAMME OF PORTSMOUTH FOOTBALL CLUB LTD.   15p

LEAGUE DIVISION THREE

**Portsmouth FC
versus
Plymouth**

Tuesday,
March 21,
1978

Kick Off 7.30 pm

Jim McCaffery

1977-78 SEASON

Only one other memory remains – one of Fred Binney's goals. As I recall, a hapless defender threw the ball back to the keeper whilst Binney was doing up his bootlaces on the edge of the box. Binney looked up and simply slotted the ball through the keeper's legs. People talk of goal poachers – Fred Binney didn't have the work ethic of a poacher.

The game ended and the rest of the family moaned. We celebrated silently. And never was a car heater more appreciated.

Mike Anderson

This was a desperate season for Argyle. We had looked dead certs to go down for so long it was untrue. Little did we know about the heroics to come. This result sparked a late-season revival, which coincided with Malcolm Allison's return to the club.

I didn't go and can tell you nothing about the game, other than that it was an evening match played mid-week. What I can tell you is that the scoreline was so unexpected it was read out from the stage during assembly the next day at school (Sutton High) to the loudest cheer I ever heard in all my time there. They never read out an Argyle score again.

Roger Willis

Argyle: Barron, Fear, Uzzell, Binney, Foster, James, Taylor, Horswill, Perrin, Megson, Bason. Sub: Trusson.

ARGYLE v. PORT VALE

Date: 29 April 1978
Location: Home Park

Football League Third Division
Attendance: 9,474

What a duff season. What a duff team. All year, it had been a grind. Argyle played the season with little style, not much conviction and, except for at the bitter end, no passion. Attendances that season were very poor.

Results had been grim. Relegation had been looming all year, but recently there had been hope. The prodigal son, in the guise of Malcolm Allison, had returned and Port Vale were to be the fatted calf slaughtered in his honour. Spurred on by a totally unexpected 5-1 away win at Pompey, there was hope where previously there had been none.

Port Vale's season had been no better than ours and, as the last couple of games approached, we had one last chance to redeem ourselves. If we beat Port Vale, we would be sure to stay up. If we lost, they would. A draw, and it was all on the last game a couple of days later at home against Bradford, who were in desperate trouble too.

At that time, it was our fairly proud boast to say we had never been in the Fourth Division. This was surely the closest to it we had ever been in our history (we could have no inkling of the horror, known as the 'McCauley years', to come).

I don't actually recall too many details of the game, other than that it was a thriller. What I do remember was the air of desperation that hung over Home Park that season. The ground seemed to be decaying in sympathy with morale. The old and, in my mind, original Devonport End had been condemned as unsafe. It was going to be demolished. Shameful really, because in those days it was in character with the Grandstand and the Lyndhurst side with its vaulted roof – unlike the backward sloping structure that eventually replaced it, with which newer generations of Greens will be familiar. The Devonport End was never quite the same again, regardless as to the opinion of its inhabitants in the twenty-odd years since.

Argyle's vocal support relocated to the Barn Park End. If you've seen the Hereford pitch invasion on TV (and I'm sure you have), when Radford scored that goal against Newcastle, then you've a good idea as to the scenes at the end. Teenage boys – myself included – streamed onto the pitch in their tight sweaters with fur-lined parka hoods flapping in their slipstream, flares flapping beneath them.

A thrilling win. Salvation and ecstasy. A positive result for either team would condemn Bradford, so they were down. They were to visit a few days later. A point would make us absolutely safe, but the job was as good as done.

Roger Willis

THE WINS AGAINST Portsmouth and Port Vale secured Argyle's Third Division status and they signed off with a 6-0 win against Bradford City. The Pilgrims finished nineteenth, with an average home crowd of just under 7,000.

Argyle 3
Johnson, Binney (2)

Port Vale 2

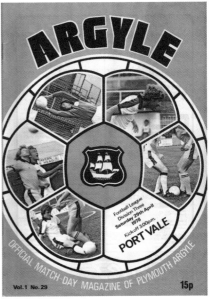

Above: Malcolm Allison celebrates the escape from relegation with the board.

Right: A tense finish to the season, but the Pilgrims survived the threat of relegation to the Fourth Division.

Below: The Green Army breathe a sigh of relief.

Argyle: Hodge, Fear, Basson, Binney, Foster, James, Taylor, Horswill, Rogers, Harrison, Perrin.

WEST BROMWICH ALBION v. ARGYLE

Date: 18 February 1984
Location: The Hawthorns

FA Cup fifth round
Attendance: 23,795

I was a student living in Gloucester at the time and set off very early. We arrived at New Street and thought about getting to the Hawthorns. A number 19 bus was the answer. I was seriously early; some Greens were already there and I joined them outside the turnstile.

Soon, a hubbub developed and everybody started peering into the distance. A woman wearing a transparent plastic mac was approaching. As she got closer, it was clear that she had forgotten to put a dress on that morning, but had compensated by donning a matching set of alluring lingerie. She wandered up and down for a while treating the good-natured badinage aimed at her with good humour. She was looking for something, I guess.

At last the turnstiles opened. I was among the first to enter the ground. I leaned on a barrier and waited, as the end filled very quickly. When a besuited Argyle came out to inspect the pitch, they were treated to a rousing reception. The away end was almost full, but the rest of the ground was empty.

Prior to the game, there was an on-pitch presentation for the newly appointed management team of Johnny Giles, Norman Hunter and Nobby Stiles. Decency prohibits repeating the chant that rang out, drowning the tannoy announcements, but suffice to say it involved Johnny Giles and his solitary pursuits!

The away end filled further; a fairly serious crush was developing. All of a sudden, there was agitation in our end. Some fans on the other side of the fence were gesticulating, chanting and trying to attract our attention. The Green Army responded angrily, but the anger quickly turned to laughs as a Union Jack with 'Swilly' emblazoned across it was raised. They were quickly transferred to our end. The crush got worse.

The game? I watched it with my arms pinned to my sides by the crowd. Argyle dominated the game to our collective delight – it was no surprise when eventually our superiority was rewarded by Tommy Tynan shinning one in at the far end. Joy was unconfined.

West Brom huffed and puffed, but they could not blow the Green house down. 1-0 was enough. I left and waited for a bus outside. I took a packet of fags from my shirt pocket for the first time in hours and looked at them, amazed. They had been totally flattened. They looked like a steamroller had gone over them.

The bus arrived. I sat on the top deck and somebody at the front had a radio tuned into Radio Two's sports report (no Five Live back then): 'The biggest upset of the day is Third Division Plymouth Argyle beating First Division West Brom'. Suddenly, the top deck was awash with green and white. We sang all the way back to the station.

New Street was chaos. There had been games that day at Birmingham City, Wolves and Villa, where they had played Leeds, Manchester United and West Ham. There had obviously been a battle. Police were everywhere. I thought I'd make myself scarce and go into Asda to buy a four pack. On the way, I bumped into a fellow Green. We hugged. His face was as manic as mine must have been. 'Yeeeeessssssss!'

West Bromwich Albion 0	Argyle 1
	Tynan

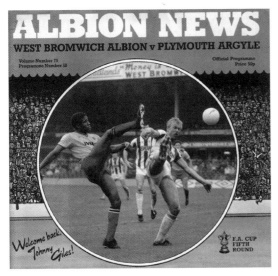

Argyle stun WBA at The Hawthorns and the cup
run really begins.

After buying the beer, I also bought a *Sports Argus*, which was the Brum version of the *Football Herald*.
'Albion Agony' was the headline. I went to my platform, read my paper and waited.

A train pulled in. A load of Welsh guys piled off and made straight for me. They had seen the paper.
'F——ing Plymouth won and Tynan scored the goal!' They were Newport fans returning from Port Vale.
Tynan, of course, had recently transferred from Newport to Argyle and Argyle had knocked Newport out
in the third round, with Tynan scoring. I kept schtum until I got back to Gloucester.

Roger Willis

Argyle: Crudgington, Nisbet, Uzzell, Harrison, Smith, Cooper, Hodges, Phillips, Tynan, Staniforth, Rogers.

DERBY COUNTY v. ARGYLE

Date: 14 March 1984   **FA Cup sixth round replay**
Location: The Baseball Ground   **Attendance:** 26,906

Where to begin? Once the final whistle was blown in the first match I knew that, no matter what, I had to go to the replay. The result was inevitable. We were going to win.

I was living in Gloucester at the time and I pondered just how I was going to get there during my journey back from the first match. Enquiries at the station revealed that going by train was easy, but return was impossible.

Returning to the halls of residence in Gloucester, the first person I saw was a girl named Helen and, joy of joys, she was emerging from a borrowed car! I had agreed to accompany her and her friend Becky on a four-legged pub-crawl as part of Rag Week. Unfortunately, the replay and the pub-crawl were on the same night.

'Fancy taking me to Derby?' I asked in blissful ignorance. 'No!' (I would be subbed by a Pompey fan named Ray – more of him later.) Plan B involved going by train and hitch-hiking back. 'If there's a God, we'll win the replay. If there's two gods I'll get home too.'

In Derby, I made for WHSmith in the town centre to find an A to Z and directions to the Baseball Ground. 'Flap, Flap, Flapper!' went out a yell from behind. 'Gibbon!' was the only reply. Classroom nicknames stick for an eternity. Gibbon had made a similar journey, but from London.

As people started to arrive for the kick-off, four dodgy-looking characters approached us. 'Where you from?' 'I'm from Gloucester, he's from London.' Best to be non-committal; violence was an intrinsic part of football in those days.

'Are you supporting Derby or Plymouth?' The speaker was a Janner. Once they heard our haphazard travel arrangements, they agreed to give us a lift back if we could find them afterwards.

The game was an amazing experience. Derby had been pants in the first game, but at home they were much better. We were under intense pressure from the off, but somehow they never looked like scoring.

There were loads of Greens there. We packed the terrace behind a goal and the fervour of the travelling support was something I had never experienced before. There were Derby fans in the tier above the terracing and they were giving it large. Warm liquid (I hope it was tea) was being thrown over us from above but most significantly of all, there was an inflatable. I forget what it was. A footballer? Snowman? Penguin? Something else? No matter. It was being dangled tantalisingly from above. Eventually they lowered it too far.

'We've got Archie Gemmill, We've got Archie Gemmill...' (not unfairly – they were about the same size). The mantra was added to the repertoire of 'Archie' songs. Somebody ripped its head off, donned it like a helmet and was raised shoulder high by the crowd. A dog ran onto the pitch. 'Archie Gemmill's girlfriend!' And so it went on. I have never seen a player take so much stick.

At some stage, Andy Rogers took a corner in front of us from the right-hand side. Cherry – spectacular in the first game – missed it. So did everyone else. The ball sailed unhindered into the side netting! 'It's a

Derby 0	Argyle 1
	Rogers

BASS OSMASTON LOWER VISITORS

DERBY COUNTY
V PLYMOUTH ARGYLE

WED 14TH MARCH 1984
KICK-OFF 7.30PM

F.A.CUP
SIXTH ROUND REPLAY

ENTER VIA TURNSTILE

41-43

THE SHAPE OF THINGS TO COME

PATRICK

RESERVED SEAT (including VAT)	Michael Dunford	ROW G
	Secretary	SEAT
£ 5.00		95

DERBY COUNTY p.l.c. | THIS PORTION TO

The Greens go to The Baseball Ground for the sixth round replay.

goal!' 'Yeeeeeeeessssssss!' Absolute mayhem. Derby attacked and attacked and attacked. The Green wall stood firm and defended the goal in front of us. All the time, we bellowed our allegiance.

The final whistle. More mayhem. Twelve Argyle players, plus the trainer and manager, celebrated in front of us. The pitch-side fence was being climbed from both sides. Johnny Hore was dancing on the pitch. Nobody wanted to leave the ground.

Eventually, we left. I bumped into my new dodgy mates and got a lift to my front door in Gloucester. Unfortunately four had grown to five and Gibbon got left behind to take his chances until the first train the next morning.

And Ray? He puked all over his feet after the second pub. The girls were not amused – they were tied to him!

Roger Willis

Argyle: Crudgington, Nisbet, Uzzell, Harrison, Smith, Cooper, Hodges, Phillips, Tynan, Staniforth, Rogers.

WATFORD v. ARGYLE

Date: 14 April 1984
Location: Villa Park

FA Cup semi-final
Attendance: 43,858

The build-up to the match was tremendous. Argyle were all over the national papers and the television, and the three of us – myself, my father and my uncle – were going to see the match of a lifetime. The semi-final of the FA Cup. We couldn't believe it. One more win and we were off to Wembley. It couldn't happen, could it?

Our League form was poor, but then what else would you expect with our cup run? We travelled by train from Plymouth to Birmingham. I remember it vividly. We took homemade pasties to eat and a pack of cards to play cribbage. When we arrived, we were policed to the match. Very good of the police, I thought, to make sure no one troubled us, and ensure we got there in time.

There was a great atmosphere at the ground, as there had been on the way there. Everyone seemed to be wearing green. We found our seats – unheard of at Home Park, as we always stood on the terracing – and enjoyed every minute of the game. The flask of scotch helped, but the cross from Barnes and the goal from Reilly failed to dampen our spirits.

We were never overawed, we were always in with a chance, and I swear that Kevin Hodges' shot was in all the way, the goalie was beaten and, to this day, I'll never understand what prevented it from nestling in the back of the net.

It was not to be. Johnny Hore had done a magnificent job, but the luck that all teams needed had deserted us. The whistle went and we returned to Plymouth, not disheartened, for we put up a good fight, but with memories that no one could take away. It's true what they say – there's nothing worse than losing an FA Cup semi-final.

James Singer

One of the things that sticks in my memory of this game was that, when the coach stopped at the motorway services, you always saw scores of people you knew from Plymouth – it seemed as though the whole city was heading to Villa Park. Old school friends, ex-work colleagues – it was virtually impossible not to see someone you knew. The atmosphere in the Holte End was brilliant and the Green Army never stopped singing.

Adrian Jones

In those days, I was a member of the London Branch and living in Tring, with Watford being the local team. We gathered at the usual meeting place near Euston Station prior to boarding the train. Well, I say train, but it must have been one that was found in a siding in the middle of nowhere. It was one of those with the corridor down one side and seating for about eight in each cage, sorry, compartment. Well there we were, seven Watford fans and me – they were all neighbours and friends from work – sharing beers and food. We were all full of expectancy.

Then the door slides open; it is a young officer from the transport police. This cannot be allowed – fans mingling and sharing beer and food – 'I must move them on'. He tries, but we ain't having it. He brings

---

Watford 1   **Argyle 0**

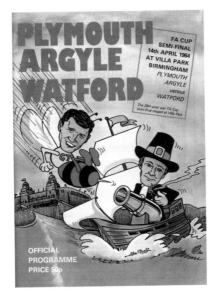

Right: The Pilgrims go to Villa Park for the FA Cup semi-final against Watford.

Far right: Tynan – Argyle's talismanic striker.

back his superior officer. After a lot of tact and diplomacy on our part, he allows us to stay together and we continue the journey to Villa Park unhindered.

The atmosphere there is great, red and yellow mixing well with green and white. George Reilly spoils the game and we head for home in the same cattle trucks, reaching our favourite location in Euston and watching *Match of the Day*.

It's Watford versus Argyle and we still lose 1-0. We head back to the hills of Hertfordshire, head held high but thumping – so near, yet so far away.

Paul Squire

I was living in Watford at the time, and a mate from Bristol and my brother, who lived in north London, were going to go together. The only train we could get to take us to Birmingham in good time from Watford left at about 10.30, but my brother couldn't possibly be there by then as he was bringing his wife's in-laws to visit her sister for the day.

I somehow managed to get tickets on their supporters' trains which would take us straight to Aston station. I had to buy the tickets from Vicarage Road and had to show the match tickets. There were a few raised eyebrows and we were advised not to show our match tickets on the train, but we got them nevertheless.

We got the train and travelled quietly and anonymously with no problem at all. My brother announced that there was no way he wanted to travel back with the Watford fans and be treated like cattle (he didn't go to many games those days), so we got a bus to New Street.

With my mate and I being students and not very well off, my brother had to pay for three singles. 'How much will it be?' he asked me. All I could say was that when I went to West Brom, the return was about £7. Imagine his shock when three singles to Watford set him back approximately £50 – and that was in 1984!

All his own fault for not being able to rouse his in-laws early enough, I say!

Andy Hutt

WATFORD v. ARGYLE

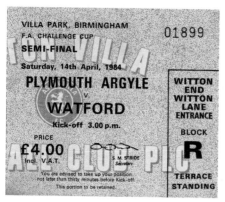

Ticket from the semi-final.

When that FA Cup run began in 1984, momentum started to gather as we drew Derby in the fourth round at Home Park and having achieved a moral victory, I decided to go to the replay at the Baseball Ground. So, I advertised on local radio that I was prepared to take three passengers in my car to the match. Within minutes I had filled two seats and then I received a call from a lady who said she had a 'boy' who'd like to go, but asked whether I would go round to her house to meet him before offering him a seat.

This seemed rather odd, but I went to her house and was introduced to a chap in his mid-twenties called Bruce. From the start, it was obvious that he was severely disabled, which didn't bother me, but she told me that he was ex-Army and had been discharged on medical grounds. It appeared that he had been involved in a bombing incident in Belfast and had been given little chance of recovery. He had had a metal plate inserted into his skull that had the effect of making it almost impossible for him to walk or talk. To add misery to his life, his parents had refused blood transfusions on religious grounds and his wife had left him, with their young son.

Having defeated the odds and survived, he was placed into the care of this lady, who specialised in caring for such unfortunate cases, and he had his own room, which was a shrine to Argyle. She told me that Argyle was his life and, despite his handicaps, he made many trips to away games under his own steam, which caused her worry and despair as it was not unusual to receive calls from the police saying that he had been picked up sleeping in a field near places like Huddersfield and thumbing lifts back to Plymouth.

The outcome was that I had no option but to give him the last seat in the car and off we headed to Derby. At that time, parking near the ground was nigh on impossible, so we had to park about a mile away and walk. Despite the fact that Bruce had a wheelchair, he adamantly refused to use it and relied instead on a walking stick. His walking was more of a stagger and we had to keep stopping for him to rest against railings and walls, but in no time the police arrived, probably having been told that a drunk had been spotted on the way to the ground. Once they realised that Bruce was not a drunk, but high on Argyle, we were bundled into the car and taken straight to the ground with the instructions that they would (and did) collect us after the game and take us back to our car.

The result is history, but on the way out of Derby Bruce hurled unintelligible abuse at the Derby fans, which was hair-raising for the rest of us.

Once tickets went on sale for the semi-final against Watford, I rang Villa Park to ask how we stood seeing as Bruce was an invalid and I was his carer. They said it was no problem, but insisted he had to be in a wheelchair to gain admittance to the ground. If nothing else, Bruce had his pride and no way was he going to use his wheelchair. After much argument, he relented and so we set off for Villa Park with the rest of the Green Army.

Once again, parking was a problem. Following another argument about using the wheelchair, Bruce finally got in it and off we set. I had never pushed a wheelchair and it quickly became obvious how difficult it was, especially amongst thousands of fans all going in the same direction.

We had managed a mile or so when we came across a zebra crossing. I was struggling to get the chair off the kerb when I spotted a group of well-bedecked Watford fans across the road. Obviously, we stood out in our scarves and suddenly they rushed across the road in our direction. As this was a time when hooliganism was still prevalent and seeing as I am built like a facing snake, I thought 'This is all I need'.

Without a word, they picked up Bruce in his wheelchair, ran across the road, dumped him down and turned to me to say 'That's all the help you'll get from Watford this afternoon', before leaving us speechless.

At the ground, we were fortunate enough to be given a seat on the cinder track next to a St John's ambulance crew, who made us welcome and praised the Argyle fans in general, saying it was the quietest and friendliest semi-final they'd ever been involved in.

On the way out of the ground, we were stopped by a lot of Watford supporters who came up to us, ruffled Bruce's scarf and hat and thanked us for a great game, which we agreed with, except for the result.

The trip home was funereal, but Bruce kept us entertained with various chants, which, by now, we had become accustomed to and could understand.

I kept in touch with Bruce for the rest of the season, but then I went to work abroad for many years and we lost touch. However, to this day, his enthusiasm, cheerfulness and high spirits, despite all his handicaps, made me very humble, grateful to have met him and proud to have been a small part of his life. Where or how he is now, I do not know, but if you read this Bruce – thank you.

Alec Henderson

THE FA CUP run had the predictable side-effect of poor results for Argyle in the Third Division, but there was a late-season rally and the Greens finished in nineteenth place. While the cup attendances had been huge, League gates averaged less than 6,000.

Argyle: Crudgington, Nisbet, Uzzell, Harrison, Smith, Cooper, Hodges, Phillips, Tynan, Staniforth, Rogers.

ARGYLE v. BRISTOL CITY

Date: 29 April 1986

Location: Home Park

Football League Third Division

Attendance: 19,900

1986 conjures up countless images of Maradona – the hand of God, his mazy run for the 'legitimate' goal against England and his celebrations after Argentina beat West Germany in the World Cup final. But for me, 1986 was all about Tynan, not Maradona.

His 10 goals in the last 9 games of the season propelled Argyle to promotion glory. What a loan spell that was. The two goals he scored – along with the other two in Argyle's demolition of Bristol City that secured promotion in 1986 – will be remembered as clearly on the day I die as on the day itself, when I was the most excited twelve-year-old in the world (well, maybe just in Elburton).

I remember being bitterly disappointed to hear on Plymouth Sound that the original match had been postponed. I was in the passenger seat of my Dad's car as we were entering the Home Park car park at the time. But in hindsight, that made this match all the more special. Not only did the timing of the match result in promotion, but it also meant it would be the last match I could attend before my family moved to Chester. What a final match it was.

Aside from the goals and the celebrations afterwards, the details of the match are a little sketchy. With striker John Clayton out injured, the Ciderman went with what I think was an attacking 4-3-3 formation with Hodges and Nelson playing either side of Tynan, and Summerfield, Matthews and Coughlin making up the three-man midfield.

We were one up after twenty-two minutes when Sir Tommy fired into the net from close range. In the second half, attacking the Devonport End, we scored 3 times in 10 minutes to destroy City – a stunning volley from Gary Nelson from the edge of the area on fifty-four minutes. Six minutes later came the third, direct from a corner by Russell Coughlin (identical to Andy Roger's effort against Derby in the classic Cup run of 1984). The final goal was a vintage Tynan diving header (a dying art) by the penalty spot in the sixty-fourth minute.

My Dad was nervously listening to his radio hoping that Wigan hadn't won. If they had, we couldn't have been promoted on the night. As the final whistle approached, hundreds of Argyle fans climbed over the perimeter fencing and waited on the touchline to pour onto the pitch in celebration. I remember my Dad turning to me looking very concerned. He thought the FA may order the game to be replayed because of the imminent pitch invasion. And when that final whistle was blown, it was some invasion. Not a blade of grass to be seen as thousands covered the hallowed turf. I was so disappointed not to be able to join them – we were in the Grandstand.

Sitting in the Grandstand, however, did bring me closer to the celebrations with the champagne spraying from the directors' box. The view from the Grandstand also made it abundantly clear that there were many more people in the ground than the 20,000 officially recorded. By all accounts it was closer to 30,000. With that crowd behind us, City never stood a chance. The crowd was packed in tight, creating a fantastic atmosphere, the likes of which just cannot be recreated in these post-Hillsborough days.

Argyle 4

Tynan (2), Nelson, Coughlin

Bristol City 0

Kevin Summerfield leads the celebrations.

Tommy scores a brace.

It really was a classic match, with all the required ingredients so often missing in the modern game – attacking wing play, great goals and passionate supporters. This match was one of the major reasons why I became so hopelessly addicted to Argyle.

For the record, Wigan drew and finished the season in fourth place. The Greens went up just behind Reading in second place, with Derby taking the last promotion place. As for the FA, my Dad needn't have worried!

Dan King

ARGYLE v. BRISTOL CITY

Above: The Home Park crowd goes mad.

Left: A glorious night for the Greens at Home Park as they secure promotion by beating Bristol City.

I had to be in Cheltenham at nine o'clock the next morning. Despite the importance of the game, I couldn't be there. What to do? That was the question. No Ceefax, Sky or Five Live in those days. The internet hadn't even been dreamt of.

The best I could do – the only football I could find – was a Welsh Cup match between Kidderminster and Newport on BBC Radio Wales. This was an MW broadcast and the signal was weak. The coverage veered unpredictably from Arabic wailing to French chat to the football commentary. At least it was football, though, and, importantly, they promised score updates from that evening's games.

The first news that I heard was that kick-off had been delayed. There was a report from their Johnnie-on-the-spot who was amazed at the size of the crowd. No further news for ages. Then 'time for the latest news from Plymouth'. I strained to hear. The 'phone rang but I ignored it. Someone else answered. There was a bang on my door. 'It's yer Mam!' She was listening to the live commentary on Plymouth Sound.

'Someone's scored! I don't know who.'

I'd guessed that much from BBC Wales. 'Who has? Is it us? What's the score?'

'I don't know. The commentator isn't making much sense. Someone's scored again!'

'Who? Who?' I was going absolutely spare.

'It's 2-0 to Argyle!'

I was going ape on the 'phone in the hall of my shared student accommodation. 'I'll ring you back later,' she said.

Back to the radio commentary.

The 'phone rang again: '3-0.' Then, '4-0.'

It all meant nothing if Wigan won.

Radio Wales: 'Wigan have a penalty. It's the last minute. If they score they will win and be promoted. If not, Plymouth… will be promoted. He's missed' (or was it saved?) 'Plymouth will be promoted. They are leading 4-0 at home to Bristol City.'

More celebrations. Off to the Beehive with my flatmates to celebrate! A wondrous occasion. I only wish that I could have been there to see it.

Roger Willis

I was sixteen, had been an Argyle fan for years and was really looking forward to this game. All my mates from school were going and I was going to go with my dad and his best mate Lockey. It was not to be. The reason – my Mum.

Basically, I had an exam to take the next day and she told me I had to stay in and revise. So I stormed up to my bedroom, slamming the door for good measure, dug out my school books and sat on my bed and thought. I then decided to open my bedroom window, as living in Peverell you can often hear the PA and crowd at Home Park, and I tuned my radio into Plymouth Sound.

I made myself comfortable, spread out my schoolbooks and sat back to listen to the legendary Ian Calvert and Tristan live from Home Park. The game started and as each goal went in, I would run downstairs to my mum to keep her updated with the game and reassure her I was actually doing some revision. Finally, the whistle blew and promotion was confirmed and being celebrated.

When I went downstairs to see mum and tell her the good news she turned around and said the worst thing she ever could have. 'Well that revision session was a complete waste of time. I should have let you go to Argyle!'

Nickie Tombs

Argyle: Crudgington, Nisbet, L. Cooper, Summerfield, Goodyear, Tynan, Hodges, Coughlin, Matthews, McElhinney, Nelson.

ARSENAL v. ARGYLE

Date: 31 January 1987

Location: Highbury

FA Cup fourth round

Attendance: 39,029

After beating Bristol City 3-1 at home in a third round replay, we were rewarded with a plum tie – Arsenal at Highbury. As we had started the new season after promotion unbelievably well, expectation of something special happening was high, and with it being pay on the day, we were unsure how many would attend.

My brother and I left Plymouth to travel to Highbury at 6a.m. on a cold but dry morning, stopping at Crediton to have some breakfast, change cars and travel up with my mate Nigel. The journey up was a breeze, Nigel having serviced the car the day before, and we arrived in London at about 11a.m. We passed, and were passed by many cars and coaches decked out in green, so the anticipation of a good crowd was looking to be right. We parked on the outskirts of London and travelled to Highbury on the tube.

On arrival at the ground, we were informed that refreshments (ale) were available inside the ground, so we paid our money and went in early. We had been allocated the old 'Clock End', and this was cordoned off into two large pens, each comfortably holding about 6,000 fans. We had been assigned one of these as Arsenal and the Metropolitan Police had expected fewer fans to show up.

After having a couple of pints in relative comfort, and relishing the atmosphere, it began to get decidedly crowded as more and more Argyle fans were being allowed into the ground. About forty-five minutes from the kick-off, there was a distinct likelihood of a major catastrophe. We were being severely crushed, and there were people screaming and crying out that we were in trouble. This was two years before Hillsborough.

Fortunately for us, common sense prevailed and the police and Arsenal made a decision to open the second penned area and allow the fans to spill into this space. This was actually against government rules, as this area was allocated as the buffer zone between both sets of fans. As we had been in the ground now for a couple of hours, we were among the first to spill into the area, and the relief from being crushed was welcome.

We immediately found a space directly in front of a crash barrier behind the middle of the goal and stayed put. You can imagine our surprise as this area began to fill and we were beginning to be in a similar situation to before. It turned out that in excess of 12,500 Argyle fans had made the trip up to Highbury, and the Arsenal people on the gate allowed them all into a space for 12,000.

The very first surprise was that Geoff Crudgington had been dropped and new signing Steve Cherry was in goal, and he was about to have a 'mare. I suspect he had nightmares about that game for many years after.

Well, what can I say, Arsenal came out with eleven internationals and played the sort of one touch passing football at pace they are famous for today. The quality of the overlapping full backs (Kenny Samson and Viv Anderson) just ripped us apart and with about ten minutes to go to half-time, we were 3-0

Arsenal 6

Argyle 1

Rowbotham

The Argyle team leave the Highbury pitch.

down and Arsenal had eased off. We had been given a fantastic footballing lesson, and it was clear how big the gulf between the First and Second Division actually was.

In the second half, the impossible happened and, after quite a good move, Darran Rowbotham drilled the ball into the net. 3-1 – we were ecstatic and began to entertain thoughts of a comeback. These were soon dispelled as Arsenal upped their game and really showed us up for what we were, scoring another three goals, before easing off once more.

Seeing a fantastic Arsenal team that included the likes of Kenny Samson, Viv Anderson, David Rocastle (RIP), Paul Davis, Tony Adams and Niall Quinn, and hearing the songs sung by the Argyle fans, 'We came all this way and got stuffed', were among the highs, as was the banter between the fans.

There were lows. Bananas were thrown every time a black player came anywhere near the Argyle fans, and we are not talking one or two, there must have been dozens thrown during the game.

Nigel had not tightened the oil filter up properly whilst carrying out the service, and it dropped off at 80mph, leaving engine oil all over the M4. Then there was a three-hour wait for a breakdown truck, before finally getting home at 5.30a.m. on the Sunday morning, having not eaten since 2p.m.

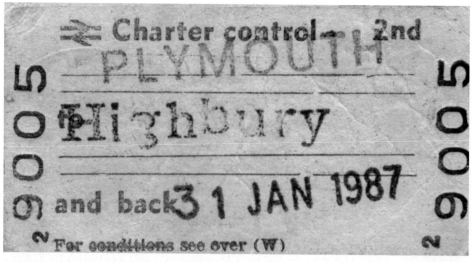

A ticket for one of the special charter trains that took the Green Army to Highbury.

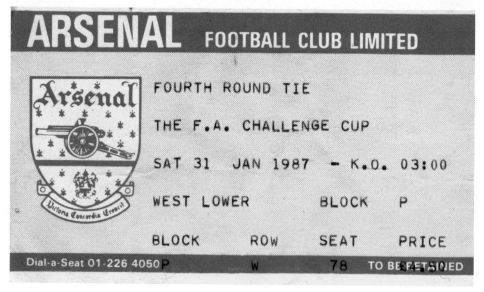

Over 12,000 Argyle fans made the journey to the League leaders, Arsenal.

In the light of the Hillsborough disaster two years later, I feel very fortunate to have survived at that game. Had the authorities not opened the second penned area, I really believe that the newspapers would have been talking about a Highbury tragedy, involving Plymouth Argyle fans, and I don't mean the final score.

Eddie Bray

Argyle: Cherry, Nisbet, L. Cooper, Clayton, Matthews, Hodges, Coughlin, Summerfield, Nelson, Burrows, Tynan.

Subs: Rowbotham, Uzzell

Portsmouth v. Argyle

Date: 20 April 1987

Location: Fratton Park

Football League Second Division

Attendance: 17,171

Wembley aside, this still rates as my all-time favourite Argyle away day. As it turned out, this was to be Dave Smith's last win of the season – a season that saw us finish in an agonising seventh spot in the Second Division after an end-of-season slump.

The reason this was so sweet was, well, it was Pompey wasn't it? Forget Exeter, these were our real rivals, and memories of 1982 at Home Park (when their fans went on the rampage) meant this was pay-back time – as far as the score was concerned, anyway.

In an age when utter contempt was prevalent for Pompey, we arrived in Fratton (what a hole) in our privately-hired coach in a boisterous mood, having been on the sauce for the duration of the journey. Attempts to persuade our driver to detour to one last watering hole had proved fruitless, and so we got off the coach, only to be herded into what was, still to this day, the biggest police escort I've ever had the misfortune to be caught up in.

One of the most vivid memories of the day was being escorted through the *Coronation Street*-style lanes, paying 'homage' to the then Pompey manager, Alan Ball. I guess you had to be there, but when you have around 200 or 300 grown men singing in the highest-pitched voices they can muster, you kind of get the picture – hilarious.

Having got onto the packed terrace with 3,000 other Greens, the vast majority of the match was a blur, apart from the moment Kevin Summerfield advanced on the 'keeper, slotted home and sank to his knees right in front of us to spark the most manic celebrations I've ever witnessed in over twenty-five years of following Argyle.

Pompey had been unbeaten at home all season up until that point, so to take their unbeaten record and keep our own promotion dreams very much alive made it a bit special.

In the end, they went up, we stayed down – que sera sera – but what a day.

PAFC Loyal

I was seventeen at the time, and this game sticks in my mind for so many reasons – the first being the transport. There were eight of us, all mates from school, all typical lads who were a bit skint, and who refused to travel with the Official Travel Club as we always liked to stop for a couple of beers on the way up (and back). We were very badly organised, yet somehow ended up winging it to more or less every away game.

For this particular game, we couldn't find a lease company willing to hire us a nice minibus, so we borrowed my neighbour's knackered old transit van. No windows in the back (anybody who broke wind was not popular!), no seats, no carpet, nothing. We sat on the metal floor for four or five hours up the coastal road to Pompey.

We got to a village outside Pompey about two hours before the game. The local police had obviously had the heads up that we were en route (flags hanging out the back door, scarves off the aerial – we were

Portsmouth 0	Argyle 1
	Summerfield

hard to miss!) and were waiting for us, but they soon realised we were no trouble, escorted us to a local 'safe' pub, and just gave us some advice on where to park in Portsmouth. We stopped there for a couple of hours, then made our way to Fratton Park.

We expected absolutely nothing out of the game itself. If I remember correctly, Pompey hadn't lost at home all season under Alan Ball and had, bar the singing, already won promotion, while we had our normal dismal away record at that time – so our hopes weren't high. But, as normal, none of that mattered, we just wanted to be part of the travelling Green Army.

It also gave me great pride to see Michael Foot standing on the terraces, smiling as always, shaking everyone's hand, mingling and chatting with his fellow Greens – what a great man! The only bit of the game I clearly remember was the goal. As I recall, there was a long punt upfield towards Summerfield, who had just come on as sub. The ball dropped out of the air, he stuck a leg out and looped it up over the keeper. We went mad, out-sung the home fans for the rest of the game, and won 1-0. Result!

The drive home was the norm at the time. Stopping off at a pub somewhere near Weymouth, performing Argyle chants every time we went through a village, falling asleep about an hour from home with a throat stripped raw from too much beer, singing and fags! Oh, to be seventeen again.

Leon Hannaford

IN THE SEASON following promotion, Argyle had held their own and finished in a healthy seventh position. Average attendances were over 12,000 as the Greens briefly threatened to finally break into the big time, but it was a step too far.

Below: Ciderman (Dave Smith) greets Kevin Summerfield as the Greens defeat Pompey again.

Right: Argyle win again at their traditional port rivals.

Far right: How the teams lined up at Fratton Park.

Argyle: Cherry, Coughlin, L. Cooper, Clayton, Law, Matthews, Uzzell, Nelson, Brimacombe, Tynan, Hodges. Sub: Summerfield

ARGYLE v. LEEDS UNITED

Date: 17 October 1987

Location: Home Park

Football League Second Division

Attendance: 9,358

I've probably seen Argyle play around 700 games in the last twenty years, from the north of Scotland to Penzance, and I can still remember the first more clearly than most: 12 September 1987, Argyle 3 West Bromwich Albion 3. Two from Tynan for us, two from a fashionably permed Andy Gray for them (whatever happened to him, I wonder?).

I had come down to the West Country a week previously to take up the post of Argyle correspondent for the *Western Morning News*, having graduated from a homely weekly newspaper based in Hitchin, the *North Herts Gazette*.

My colleagues on the *Gazette* – a great bunch of truly talented journos – found it amusing that I was going to cover a club whose manager did not appear to be fully acquainted with his own side's performances (following Dave Smith's memorable lapse of memory at Reading when he missed Gary Peters' own-goal winner for us).

Notwithstanding what, even to a rookie reporter like me, was a worrying lack of tactical nous, the Ciderman had managed to steer us to the summit of the late 1980s equivalent of the Coca-Cola Championship. On the day I travelled from the Home Counties to Home Park they were away at second-placed Barnsley in what was, frankly, an unlikely top-of-the-table clash.

As I reached the edge of Devon in my Mini Cooper, I tuned the car radio to BBC Radio Devon for commentary on the match. Within seconds of locating the correct frequency, Barnsley scored, and the Tykes went on to win the game. Argyle went on the sort of run that was to become familiar to me over the years. Including the drama of my 'real' debut against WBA, they lost 4 and drew 3 of their next 7 games.

It all got a bit too much for Smith, who decided that the visit of Billy Bremner's Leeds on 17 October was not a bad time to go on a scouting mission. Martin Harvey, his right-hand man – 'Harve' to everyone and extremely popular with the dressing-room – was left holding what many saw as a poisoned chalice.

I was waiting for my first win, Argyle were waiting for their first in ten, and no one expected them to get it with a side that had conceded 19 goals in the previous 8 matches.

For the first time, but definitely not the last in two decades of watching the Greens professionally, they failed to live up to expectations. The defence, though, did not let anyone down – except themselves, again. Within eighteen minutes, they had conceded two more goals. The only difference this time was that we had already scored twice, through John Clayton and Kevin Summerfield – a man surely far too thin to be a professional footballer.

Clearly, Argyle needed to be defending as little as possible if they were to win the game, and, thus, by the simple expediency of attacking at every opportunity, they not only kept the ball out of their net but went on to score three more times: Summerfield and Clayton again, and centre-back Mark Smith – who can forget Smudger's celebrations?

Argyle 6

Clayton (2), Summerfield (2), Smith, Tynan

Leeds United 3

Above: A glorious result for the Pilgrims.

Right: The Greens go goal crazy as they beat Leeds United 6-3 at Home Park.

Leeds did pull a goal back, but Argyle made the game thoroughly safe, despite their own defence's profligacy, when Tommy Tynan added a sixth (eight goals scored previously and none of them claimed by the Tank – surely a record?).

All this with the Ciderman nowhere in sight (rather like for Peters' goal). After the match, I was given an insight into the mood of the dressing-room. 'Good result,' chirruped this greenhorn Green reporter to one of the principal Pilgrims. 'We did it for Harve,' he growled back at me. Welcome to the world of professional football.

I'm lucky that TSW covered the game, meaning Pete Barraclough's measured commentary and the Pilgrims' appealing six are preserved forever.

Wonder if Smithy ever watched it?

Rick Cowdery

ARGYLE FINALLY FINISHED in sixteenth place in the Second Division, watched by Home Park crowds of over 10,000.

Argyle: Crudgington, J. Rowbotham, L. Cooper, Matthews, Law, Smith, Hodges, Summerfield, Tynan, Clayton, Brimacombe. Sub: D. Rowbotham

Argyle v. Everton

Date: 28 January 1989

Location: Home Park

FA Cup fourth round

Attendance: 27,566

The fourth round cup tie against Everton at Home Park in January 1989 was a taste of the big time. We were on *Match of the Day*, playing one of the biggest teams in the country. Back then, seeing your ground on the telly was still a big deal.

Even watching the recording now, it looks like a match from further back than the late 1980s, with the swaying, swarming masses on the terraces, their dark winter clothes splashed with outbreaks of green and white. I had grown up believing that games like this were the epitome of the 'romance of the cup'.

I huddled onto the Mayflower terrace with my Dad, brother, and a sea of others, straining to see the action, and for once recognising every opposition player. That was worrying.

Ken Brown's team were, of course, showered in clichés by the media: the plucky underdogs, great cup run in 1983/84, footballing outpost, they play in green don't you know, ad infinitum. I would get used to this over the years. The other focuses of media attention were two talismanic players in the Argyle team at the time, Tommy Tynan and Alan Miller.

Miller was in the latter part of a sparkling loan period from Arsenal. The young man with the spiky mullet (I sported a similar hairstyle at the time) had put in some eye-catching performances behind a leaky back four and midfield that kept him busy as he covered for the injured Steve Cherry.

Meanwhile, up front we were witnessing imperial phase Tynan. He had banged in four against Blackburn at Home Park back in November, and would end the season with 26 goals. The outstanding moments that stay with me from that afternoon are the chants of 'Tynan is better than Cottee' and 'Miller is better than Southall'.

A crowd of nearly 28,000 swept the team along, rather than overwhelming the players, who were used to less than 9,000 on most home Saturdays. We matched the First Division side for most of the game. There was little to choose between the teams as we made it to half-time at 0-0.

I expected Everton to take the lead and then sit on it, but it was Argyle who went in front on sixty-two minutes. A long ball forward was held up by McCarthy, who turned and spread the ball wide to Mark Stuart, the archetypal tricky winger. Stuart surged into the area, but his cross to the far post eluded Tynan. Kevin Hodges raced in to save the ball from going dead, and the cross was only half punched away by Southall, straight to the oncoming McCarthy. His half-volley evaded men on the line and ignited the terraces.

At the time, I thought Kevin Sheedy was overrated. I don't remember him contributing much as an attacking force that day as Kenny Brown and Kevin Hodges on the Argyle right kept him in check. But he had his say with around ten minutes to go.

As seems to be the way with the big teams in such games, Everton won a debatable penalty. A hand ball was given against Adrian Burrows in a penalty area melee. Few players appealed, but the referee saw something. It looked questionable to us, but then it would. Replays showed that it was ball onto hand as Burrows was knocked off-balance in a four-man challenge. There was nothing he could do about it. No matter.

Argyle 1

McCarthy

Everton 1

Above left: Sean McCarthy scores.

Above right: The team savour the moment.

Left: First Division Everton come to Home Park for a fourth round FA Cup tie.

Far left: Ticket from the match.

Sheedy stepped up to smash home the penalty past Miller. The Everton no.11 celebrated with gusto. It rankled. Yes Kevin, you and your highly paid, internationally-capped mates have scraped a jammy equaliser against Plymouth. It still rankles.

Of course, we were stuffed in the replay and the almost heroic first game has been forgotten outside Plymouth. Is that the romance of the cup?

Toby Jones

IN AN INDIFFERENT season, League and FA Cup games against Everton and Manchester City provided a distraction from poor League results, which saw Argyle finish in eighteenth place in the Second Division.

Argyle: Miller, Burrows, Marker, Smith, Hodges, Tynan, McCarthy, Summerfield, Uzzell, Stuart, Brown.

ARGYLE v. ARSENAL

Date: 3 October 1989   Football League Cup second round (second leg)
Location: Home Park   **Attendance:** 17,360

Whilst sat amongst the other 5,000 obsessives watching a rather dour Carling Cup game against Peterborough United, my mind was cast back to the days when England's third competition actually meant something. The final, shown live on ITV in those days before being whisked off to Sky, would attract a build-up – and an audience – to rival the FA Cup itself.

Nowadays, the competition has the deserved reputation of being a proverbial pain in the backside – a two-bob, run-of-the-mill, hum-drum, Mickey Mouse event. But there was a time when even the cream of English football took it seriously – and that meant fielding their strongest XI.

So it was no surprise that Argyle came into this second leg two goals behind – a cagey performance by the Gunners, but surely their stubborn defence and lethal counter-attack would be enough to see them home? But it wasn't going to be as simple as that. Not for the first fifteen minutes, anyway.

Argyle spent the first quarter of an hour huffing, puffing and roughing up the opposition. You never know with these games – two quick goals and sufficient time wasting thereafter would take us nicely to a penalty shoot-out. But all such ideas were put on the back-burner when the late, great David Rocastle's shot rifled off David Byrne and into the top corner of the net. Suddenly Argyle needed four against the reigning Barclays First Division champions – and the best defence in England. A comeback now would be a product of Hollywood.

Nevertheless, Argyle rallied. Tommy Tynan pounced to slam home from close range, and we were level with the champions. Moments later, Tynan turned supplier, only for Clayton's shot to be saved by John Lukic. Were Argyle turning a corner? Were we going to make a game of this?

No. Arsenal went 2-1 up before the break, threw on the ridiculously fast Perry Groves, and the rest is history. The Arsenal machine moved effortlessly through the gears. Four goals were scored in quick succession as they proved why they were the current champions. Groves, Alan Smith, Rocastle again and Michael 'Sumo' Thomas grabbed the goals. Arsenal ran out 8-1 aggregate winners. So much for the 'romance' of the cup.

My personal memory of this match is not entirely happy. Being in the Devonport End with an Arsenal-besotted father, and wondering how long he would keep chanting for his team before taking one in the face, is an experience no boy of eight should be put through.

Andrew Owen

ANOTHER HIGH-PROFILE League Cup game lightened a poor season for the Greens who ended the term in eighteenth place in the Second Division. Average home attendances had dropped to less than 9,000.

Argyle 1   **Arsenal 6**
  Tynan

For the second time in two seasons Argyle face Arsenal.

Argyle: Wilmot, Brown, Brimacombe, Marker, Burrows, Morrison, Hodges, Byrne, Tynan, Campbell, Stuart. Subs: Thomas, Pickard.

ARGYLE v. BLACKBURN ROVERS

Date: 2 May 1992
Location: Home Park

Football League Second Division
Attendance: 17,459

Argyle were fourth from bottom going into this game. A win would guarantee safety, anything less and we would be relying on other results. Blackburn also needed three points to secure a play-off place. A crowd of 17,500 flowed into Home Park, where attendances had not managed to break into five figures all season, despite the arrival of our new high-profile manager. Such a novelty led to a fifteen-minute delay for the kick-off.

In his thirteen games in charge, Peter Shilton had managed to coax just four wins and two draws to add to our measly points total. You can have all the media attention and big name enthusiasm in the world, but if the team is low on confidence and even lower on ability, and the manager is a first-timer, it's an unlikely combination for survival.

Shilton had inherited Dave Kemp's long ball, goal shy, defensively shaky band of Wimbledon cast-offs, along with inexperienced local youngsters and Dwight Marshall. Shilton himself had taken over in the Argyle goal from the unfortunate Rhys Wilmot. It was still less than two years since Shilton had helped England to the World Cup semi-final with some fine performances, and he had shown flashes of the glory days in the season run-in. But the ageing limbs and slower reactions bestowed by age were cruelly exposed in this most vital of matches.

Argyle had been the first opponents of the Kenny Dalglish-era Blackburn back in October and the Greens had been thumped 5-2 amid intense media interest, which included a spot on the BBC News. Dalglish had since led his team to the edge of the play-offs, but the strugglers took the lead after just twelve minutes in the regular season's final game.

Marker worked the ball from the corner flag inside to David Smith, whose shot from just inside the right edge of the area squeezed under Bobby Mimms. Exactly the sort of help Argyle needed. The rest of the first half was fairly tentative, and you felt that Argyle had scored too early. To hold on until half-time would have been a huge boost. That wasn't to be.

The executioner of Plymouth's survival hopes was David Speedie, an astonishingly unpopular player notorious for being booed by his own fans on occasion during his career. He was a mouthy, aggressive, arrogant little man on the football pitch. Unfortunately, he was also a damn fine player, quick, skilful, with sharp awareness, great in the air for a short bloke, and a decent finisher.

A few minutes before half-time, a long punt from Colin Hendry caught Marker flat-footed and the onrushing Speedie lashed the dropping ball into the net. Then, three minutes into first-half injury time, and with Argyle still recovering, Speedie delivered the body blow.

A Blackburn corner found its way back to Scott Sellars but his left-wing cross was misjudged and flapped at feebly by Shilton. The ball homed in on Speedie's balding head and it was 2-1 to the visitors right in front of the Devonport End. The confidence drained from Argyle, and the men from Jack Walker's bank account controlled the second half.

Argyle 1
  Smith

Blackburn Rovers 3

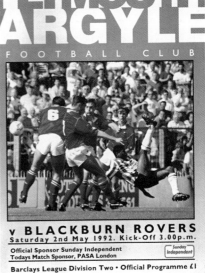

v **BLACKBURN ROVERS**
Saturday 2nd May 1992. Kick-Off 3.00p.m.
Official Sponsor Sunday Independent
Todays Match Sponsor, PASA London

Barclays League Division Two • Official Programme £1

Above: A relegation decider as Kenny Dalglish and Blackburn Rovers come to Home Park.

Left, above: Mickey Evans tussles with Colin Hendry.

Left, below: Ticket from the match.

The almost inevitable third goal on the break came after sixty-seven minutes. A perfect Cowans through ball caught the Argyle defence square, and Speedie raced into the box before planting a low shot inside Shilton's near post. Game over. The final twenty minutes or so were spent listening to the radio, hoping for a minor miracle. Oxford now only needed a draw to overhaul us, but they got an unlikely 2-1 win at Tranmere.

We were down. Most of us knew it at half-time. It didn't feel like one of those gut wrenching, 'if only' style disasters when the final whistle blew, but rather a confirmation of season-long suspicions. Fanciful dreams of a great escape had been dashed.

Blackburn finished sixth and then beat Leicester in the play-off final, and have barely looked back since. Argyle took twelve years to get back to the start again.

Toby Jones

Argyle: Shilton, McCall, Morrison, Smith, Garner, Evans, Lee, Marker, Morgan, Cross, Marshall. Subs: Fiore, Nugent.

ARGYLE v. EXETER CITY

Date: 10 April 1993

Location: Home Park

Football League Second Division

Attendance: 9,391

The last few years have been kind to Argyle. So kind that some fans take our fantastic rise up the divisions in recent times for granted. Any such fan questioning the players, management style or board needs to be sat down and reminded about a time when things really weren't so rosy – and what better game to encapsulate that than this one? This was a game so embarrassing that hundreds vowed never to return to Home Park afterwards.

There are three swear words around Home Park – phrases that one dare not use for risk of having people glance hatefully in their direction – 'Dan McCauley', 'Exeter City', 'That Game'.

I'm not going to throw any funny anecdotes or witty quotes in your direction, there was absolutely nothing in the slightest bit comical about the build-up, the game or the result.

The game itself? Fairly entertaining for the neutral, as the cliché goes. Exeter City fans must have been delighted to have travelled such a short distance for such a comfortable game. Argyle played with no passion, no spirit, no skill, no discipline and no desire. Exeter City played with passion and that was all anyone needed against this pathetic rabble.

Walking home, I was reminded of the result many, many times by passing cars. At the time, it was not the in thing to support Argyle. Everyone in Plymouth loved Manchester United, and what better way to justify their armchair support than by pointing this scoreline out to us, and asking 'Give me one good reason to support Argyle?'

And for the time, they were right. There was no good reason. *Dad's Army* was on that evening, and Fraser's immortal catchphrase 'we're doomed' seemed to ring more true than ever.

So let this serve as a lesson to all those who moan about the colour of the season-ticket jacket or to those who complain that the ticket line is busy. As Harold Macmillan once said, 'You've never had it so good'.

Andy Owen

After having 'Alan Ball's a w——er, he wears a w——er's hat' sung at him for most of the game, Bally promptly threw his hat in the air when City scored their third, only for it to be blown into the Mayflower – needless to say, it wasn't returned! Despite the lack of colour clash, the ignominiousness of the day was summed up by the fact that we were beaten by a team wearing a hideous purple and yellow away kit. Painful. Just painful.

Andy Chapman

Argyle 0

Exeter City 3

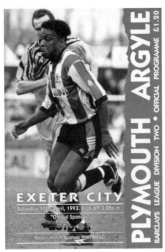

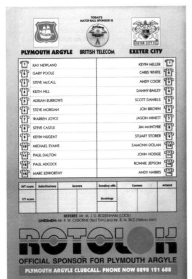

Above left: The Pilgrims are humbled.

Above right: A definite low point as the Grecians easily beat Argyle at Home Park.

Left: How the two Devon teams lined up.

Argyle: Newland, Nugent, Boardman, Castle, Joyce, McCall, Hill, S. Morgan, Dalton, Poole, Morrison. Subs: Evans, Barlow

WEST BROMWICH ALBION v. ARGYLE

Date: 12 April 1993
Location: The Hawthorns

Football League Second Division
Attendance: Attendance: 16,130

This was the only season I spent as an exile living in Manchester. A call to the Northern Branch put me in touch with other Green obsessives and the tour to nearly thirty games was on.

The season was a huge disappointment with Shilton's expensively assembled squad failing to click, the undoubted low point being the 3-0 humiliation by squeaky Ball's Exeter at Home Park on the Easter Saturday.

So it was with no great enthusiasm that I met up with my northern branch lift back 'oop north' via The Hawthorns on the following Bank Holiday Monday. To make matters worse, we had been roped into a supporters' five-a-side match and so had to leave at 7a.m.

The solemn mood of the drive up was relieved upon arrival at Junction 2 of the M5, where the farcical attempts to get the combined northern and Avon branch vehicles into a convoy with our WBA escort resembled a Keystone Cops movie. The embarrassment of this was dwarfed when it turned out we were supposed to be playing eleven-a-side. The Argyle 'team' was only identifiable by the mixture of green jerseys hiding beer bellies, while the Albion lads, who played in a local league, had fully numbered Baggies kits.

Luckily, our hosts took the mix-up in good humour, so we abandoned the game and proceeded straight to their local. West Brom were riding high in the League that season and the locals were confident of a five or six goal mauling by Osvaldo Ardiles' team. Tales of Nicky Marker cutting short Ossie's Blackburn debut raised spirits along with the local mild ale. It was only the designated driver's threats to leave us in Brum that persuaded me going to the game was a better option than staying in the pub.

A few hundred Argyle fans were scattered across the vast expanses of the old Smethwick End terrace and it was lucky the sun was shining, as the roof had been condemned and removed like the Dem'port ten years before. Before kick-off, few of the travelling faithful felt like trying to out-sing the 16,000 Baggies, in contrast with my only previous trip there in 1984. Come to think of it, the noise from the Green Army when Tommy scored that day probably caused the damage to the roof!

The game started much as feared with Bob Taylor tapping in from close range within the first ten minutes and the fans slumped over crush barriers, expecting the worst. Soon after, though, wing-wizard Paul Dalton found space on the left and sent over a hanging cross which Steve Castle met with a towering header after a trademark late run. The baying Baggies fans were silenced and were soon completely stunned when Martin Barlow sent over a cross, which Castle stooped low down to meet at the near post and put Argyle into an amazing lead.

Argyle held onto the lead until half-time by the width of the woodwork, as Taylor crashed a thunderbolt volley against the crossbar. Whether Argyle could hold out against the inevitable second-half onslaught was the main question at half-time.

The WBA keeper came for a high ball and ended up in the 'D' with the ball still in his gloves. This was before the days of the 'professional foul', so he stayed on the pitch, but was helpless to stop Castle completing his hat-trick with a strike in the style later patented by Paul Wotton.

West Bromwich Albion 2

Argyle 5

Castle (3), Dalton, Barlow

West Bromwich Albion v. Argyle

From the ridiculous to the sublime – Argyle hit back to win 5-2 at The Hawthorns.

Argyle were purring, with the peerless Steve McCall giving the control in midfield to allow Castle to continue wreaking havoc. Another free-kick in a similar position had the wall cowering, which was all the invitation Dalton needed to curl the ball into the bottom corner. Castle again unleashed a rocket, which was blocked but fell to Barlow, who turned this way and that before slotting home.

The home fans left in their droves with many missing their consolation goal. We cheered ironically and scaled the safety fences to herald our team. After the match, we continued north with scarves flying and strained voices singing.

Surely this was it, an Argyle team who would sweep away all who stood before them next season.

Stuart Caskey

ARGYLE FINISHED IN mid-table, settling for fourteenth place at the end of the season. Home Park saw average attendances fall to less than 6,000.

Argyle: Newland, Nugent, Barlow, Castle, Evans, McCall, Hill, S. Morgan, Dalton, Poole, Morrison.

Exeter City v. Argyle

Date: 2 March 1994
Location: St James' Park

Football League Division Two
Attendance: 6,601

Unbelievably, this win was Argyle's first at St James' Park in over sixty years. Early on in the game, the City fans taunted us with chants of 'You'll never beat the City', and 'We beat the scum 5-0', referring to their double over us the previous season, which included a humiliating 3-0 defeat at Home Park. As a teenager, supporting Argyle but living in Exeter at the time, the games against City were the be-all and end-all for me, and I dreaded losing them. Watching Peter Shilton's expensively assembled team put in such a gutless performance is still probably my lowest point in nearly twenty years of following the Greens. 'Gutted' is an overused term in football, but it describes how I felt after that game.

Surely this time it would be different? In the 1993/94 season, we were playing the best football I've ever seen from an Argyle side. The previous season, Shilton had seemed baffled by the importance the fans placed upon the derby games, and that attitude was surely passed on to the players, contributing to their poor performance. By this game, he was in no doubt about what was required. The signs weren't promising though, as City had won 1-0 at Home Park in the Autoglass Trophy earlier in the season and Dwight Marshall and Paul Dalton were unavailable.

Argyle had the best early chances and should have taken the lead, but when Mark Cooper – always one of my most hated City players – scored in the twenty-eight minute with a deft back-heel, the feeling in the away end was one of 'here we go again'. As he turned in celebration, someone from the away end hurled a toilet roll at Cooper, but like the chances Argyle had spurned so far in the game, it was narrowly off target. The rest of the first half continued in the same vein. With Steve McCall controlling the midfield against former Pilgrim Russell Coughlin, and Micky Evans winning his battle with another ex-Argyle player, Robbie Turner, Argyle were passing the ball well and creating good opportunities, but failing to take them.

In the forty-eighth minute, however, we were back on level terms. Kevin Nugent played the ball to Mark Patterson on the right-hand side, just inside the Exeter half. Patterson played a one-two with Wayne Burnett, skipped past three challenges and fired the ball across the six-yard box, where it was gloriously turned into his own net by Mark Gavin. The away end went crazy. So much confetti had been thrown from our end that it had formed drifts behind Peter Fox's goal, yet even more of it was thrown into the air and on the pitch. It was apparent that at least half of the Grandstand, and a good proportion of people in the home end opposite us, were celebrating as well, which caused the Exeter fans in the 'Cowshed' to call for the police to 'Get the Argyle off the Bank'. Soon a line of yellow police were mobilising to quell any threat of trouble.

Three minutes later we were celebrating again. When Micky Evans nimbly evaded a challenge (honestly!) and got to the by-line, his low cross fell to Burnett on the edge of the box, and he coolly side footed it into the corner. More bedlam in the away end. Never has 'You're not singing anymore' sounded so sweet!

Exeter City 2

Argyle 3
o.g., Burnett, Evans

Trigger celebrates as Argyle
win at St James' Park.

Even though we continued to take the game to City after we'd scored, I couldn't relax. In my mind, we would still somehow manage to throw the game away and lose 3-2, and the grief from my school mates would be even worse! Then, just when I was worrying that we were going to regret our missed chances, Micky capped his Man of the Match performance with the third goal. Patterson threw the ball to Nugent, who turned his marker and played the ball in low to the near post for Trigger to crash it into the roof of the net.

3-1 to the Greens – surely that was game over? Almost. City were given a lifeline when poor defending by Argyle, the sort that would eventually undermine our promotion chances, gave a chance to David Adekola, who turned and shot from close range. There were a few scares for us before the end, especially in the very last second when Alan Nicholls decided to push an Exeter player over in the penalty area, even though the ball was going out for a goal kick. But then the referee blew the final whistle and it was all over.

Argyle fans ran onto the pitch from three sides of the ground, first trickling over the barriers, then hundreds pouring out to congratulate the team. Some made a charge for the Big Bank to gloat at the City fans, but the police soon stopped them. I stayed in the away end, with my arms aloft and a huge grin on my face. I was still grinning when I got home that night. In fact, I couldn't get to sleep because I couldn't stop grinning. When I went into school the next day, instead of saying anything to my mates to rub it in, I carried on grinning, which wound them up even more. I'm grinning now just remembering it! We've had more comprehensive wins over City since then, and more dramatic ones as well, but none that have matched the feeling I had after that game. We'd finally done 'em, and it felt bleddy brilliant.

Paul Mitchelmore

Argyle: Nicholls, Patterson, Naylor, Hill, Comyn, McCall, Burnett, Castle, Nugent, Skinner, Evans. Sub: McCarthy

Hartlepool United v. Argyle

Date: 7 May 1994
Location: Victoria Park

Football League Division Two
Attendance: 2,382

The game of football never ceases to amaze. There we were, over 400 miles from home, somewhere south of Newcastle, watching our team put on (mathematically, at least) their finest show since my granddad was a twinkle in the postman's eye.

Shilton's side had put together a fine season, but were lagging behind Reading, already promoted as champions, and Port Vale, who just needed to beat Brighton to gain promotion. Argyle had to beat Hartlepool and we hoped against all hope that Albion would do us a favour. Hartlepool United were already relegated and had nothing to play for – an attitude the home fans had certainly taken heed of – less than 2,000 of them bothered to turn up.

With heads firmly glued to portable radios, the game commenced. The first half moved along nicely – Argyle put four goals past the hapless 'Pool defence and were pretty much home and dry by half-time. Such a scoreline would normally bring a grin to my face, but my radio informed me that Vale were a goal up. Word quickly got around.

Cue the strangest forty-five minutes of football I think I've ever witnessed (only surpassed by the home match against Chesterfield in 2004). Argyle continued ripping shreds into Hartlepool's defence. 6-0 up away from home, but the travelling support were not the raucous bunch they should have been. Why? Vale were two up.

Hartlepool finally realised that they were also permitted to partake in the beautiful game, and crafted a goal of their own. 6-1. Still the atmosphere was below par. Brighton had scored, but Port Vale had quickly put the game (and the promotion race) beyond any doubt by taking a third.

Most of us, watching solemnly and contemplating the dreaded lottery of the play-offs, cheered as Richard Landon completed his hat-trick and made it 8-1, Argyle's joint biggest ever victory and the biggest scoreline in all four divisions for the season.

This spectacle finally drew to a close with Argyle embarrassing their hosts, but there was a feeling of frustration in the air all afternoon. Argyle's record victory, coupled with some of the best football ever seen at Home Park, had culminated in the 'reward' of a trip to Burnley. Football has its highs and lows. On this day, we tasted the extremes of both.

Andy Owen

This is the match I always think of when people mention Alan Nicholls. With Argyle six goals to the good, young Alan was on good bantering form, baiting the Hartlepool fans and then turning round and holding up six fingers in response to our chant of 'Nicholls, what's the score?'

Unfortunately, at that exact moment, Hartlepool mounted their only successful attack of the entire game – Nicholls turned round to discover a Hartlepool player suddenly bearing down on goal and about to shoot. He dived quickly to his right and blocked the shot – his reactions were that good – but he

---

Hartlepool United 1

Argyle 8
Marshall, McCall, Landon (3), Dalton (2), Castle

A record win for Argyle, but they are denied automatic promotion.

Above left: Alan Nicholls, fresh from the victory, attempts to drive the team coach home after Nigel Springthorpe asks him what he intends to do for a living when he finishes his playing career.

Above right: Ticket from the match.

couldn't hold it and another Hartlepool player, Nicky Peverell, knocked in the rebound. Alan got up off the turf, went straight over to Peverell and shouted 'w——er!' in his face.

A good half of the entire away end seemed to collapse with laughter, and someone started a chant of 'We only sing when it's 6-0'.

Drew Savage

Argyle: Nicholls, Burrows, Marshall, Hill, Comyn, McCall, Castle, Patterson, Landon, Dalton, Barlow. Sub: Naylor.

ARGYLE v. BURNLEY

Date: 18 May 1994

Location: Home Park

Football League Division Two play-off semi-final

Attendance: 17,515

There was certainly some over-confidence sloshing around Home Park leading up to kick-off in the play-off game versus Burnley. This foolishness was based on our ten-man 0-0 draw in the away leg, married to our uninhibited attacking verve that had delivered 88 goals during the season. The press had written off Burnley. We had finished 12 points above them. The more seasoned and cynical among us were worried that Argyle would find a way to mess it up.

While the day-trippers prepared for an outing to Wembley, the rest of us carried bags of nerves and anticipation into the ground. We were a thunderously entertaining side back in 1993/94. Peter Shilton had assembled a team with flair, imagination, and more skill than he had mortgages. The line-up included names that will conjure dewy-eyed reminiscence in generations to come: Castle, Dalton, Marshall, McCall, Nicholls, Patterson. The missing man that night was striker Kevin Nugent, who had been injured and replaced by Richard Landon towards the end of the season. Landon, inexperienced and lacking the awareness and touch of Nugent, kept his place after scoring five times in the goal-rich run-in.

The team was unchanged. The strip wasn't. Another ghost that ageing Argyle supporters will summon from these play-offs is the cursed green and black home strip introduced for this game. A great looking strip forever tarnished by play-off defeat and then relegation. However, while our attacking was brash and bold, defence often seemed a secondary concern. Argyle had conceded plenty of goals that season. They sorely needed a strong centre half.

But we could outscore opponents and we had Alan Nicholls in goal – a flawed young man but an exceptional keeper, better than a Shilton well past his best. There was some fragility to the side, no question, but a final-day 8-1 stuffing of Hartlepool and the stoic draw in the first leg meant we were flying.

Not much had happened when Argyle took the lead in the fifteenth minute, Dwight Marshall lashing the ball into the roof of the net in front of the Burnley fans after a Dalton free kick. 1-0 and we were barely out of second gear, yet Argyle never found their rhythm as Burnley packed the midfield, denying Plymouth time and space.

Up front, without Nugent to link the play and create space, there were few opportunities. At the other end John Francis was a winger-cum-striker whose pace and strength exposed the soft underbelly of the Argyle defence. Comyn and Hill were decent footballers, but neither had the qualities to fend off Francis that night. Francis was allegedly the target of racist chanting that evening, and maybe that spurred him on, but the sight of a retreating, unprotected defence was all the incentive he needed.

After twenty-nine minutes a hopeful forward lob saw Comyn stutter around on toblerone boots while Francis stormed through to beat the advancing Nicholls. Two minutes later he repeated the dose. This time Francis picked the ball up just inside the Argyle half, Comyn fell over, Hill was outpaced and out-fought, and the lone striker cut across field to slot past Nicholls again.

Argyle 1

Marshall

Burnley 3

  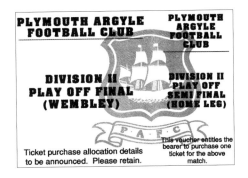

Above left: Argyle's hopes fade as Adrian Burrows is sent off in the first leg.

Above middle: Play-off agony for the Pilgrims as Burnley win 3-1 at Home Park.

Above right: Play-off final vouchers were handed out at the match – they were not needed.

The stuffing seemed to have been knocked out of Home Park, players and fans alike. Argyle fought back in the second half but rarely threatened. Nugent replaced Landon and Argyle started to string some moves together and find their feet, but it was all way, way too late. On eighty-one minutes a long kick found former Argyle midfielder Warren Joyce, who shifted it wide to Ted McMinn. He cut inside and unleashed a shot which Nicholls should have held. He spilled it – and with it Argyle's promotion destiny – and Joyce was there to ram it home.

The whistle came mercifully about ten minutes later. Emptiness. Utter, desolate emptiness. I've never felt quite like that before or since. I don't remember applauding in consolation, or being angry, just nothing. Other relegations or defeats have been painful but were generally the reward for being no good. On this occasion, a thing of footballing beauty had been crushed. The lights went out after this game, for a long time.

Toby Jones

I was a steward in the Barn Park/Mayflower corner of the ground, in the old dug-out where the St John's Ambulance volunteers sat. It was hard to contain my excitement when Dwight scored the opener, but even harder to have to stand with the Burnley fans at the end of the game, having witnessed their side win and thereby break thousands of hearts at Home Park. After the Argyle faithful had filtered out, the Burnley fans stayed on the pitch to greet their team. All the joy around me was like a stab in the heart. I had to stand there for what seemed like hours. Ghosts still need to be laid to rest on this game.

Andy Laidlaw

Argyle: Nichollls, Patterson, McCall, Hill, Comyn, Burnett, Barlow, Castle, Landon, Marshall, Dalton. Subs: Naylor, Nugent.

ARGYLE v. BRENTFORD

Date: 13 August 1994

Location: Home Park

Football League Division Two

Attendance: 7,976

Question: How long is a piece of rope?

Answer: As long as the executioner wants it to be.

It looked like the Division Two hangman had cut us plenty of slack when debutant Peter Swan put Argyle ahead just before the midway point in the first half, but then things started to go sadly wrong.

You could sense the noose tightening already as Argyle crashed 5-1 to a team who could hardly be classed as one of the Football League's giants. They went on to beat us 7-0 at their place and finish second, while Argyle finished twenty-first and crashed through the trap door to the bottom division.

Swan went from hero to villain in the space of one game, and cheers turned to jeers as Argyle's defence, supposedly strengthened by their £350,000 record signing, evaporated in the August heat. Sadly, things went from bad to worse, as we also lost 5-1 against Bradford in our next home game.

Although the details remain sketchy years later, many people remember enough to know that it was Swan who was to blame – especially this young whippersnapper, who was too young to seek solace in the consolation of a pint at the time. The heavy defeats and a 4-2 win at Stockport aside, the results from that season generally blend into an unpleasant and scarcely memorable mixture of defeats and boring draws.

And it was only the presence of the striker-turned-defender who was finally shipped off to arch rivals Burnley at the end of the season that allows me to recall this painful period. Rarely before had I found it constructive to boo a player at Home Park in the hope that it would give him a kick up the backside.

Argyle definitely went down the swannie that season, going through four managers as they slowly climbed the steps to the scaffold. And just think, for twenty or so minutes in this then seventeen-year-old's eyes, it was all going so well.

Jim Brock

Argyle 1

Swan

Brentford 5

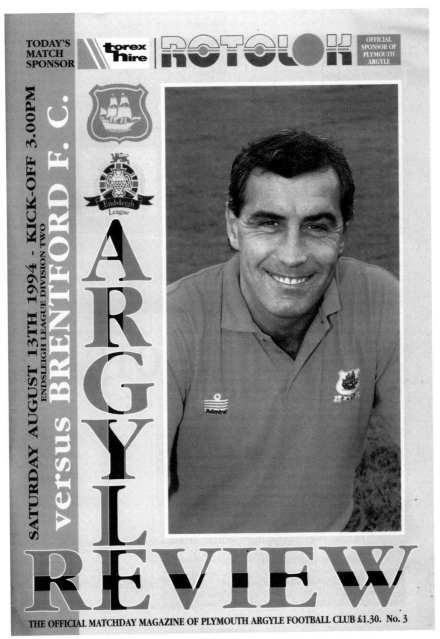

Peter Shilton smiles on the cover as the season begins, but it is not a winning start.

Argyle: Hodge, Patterson, Hill, Comyn, Swan, Payne, Barlow, Burnett, Nugent, Evans, Skinner. Subs: Edworthy, Landon.

BRENTFORD v. ARGYLE

Date: 17 December 1994

Location: Griffin Park

Football League Division Two

Attendance: 4,492

Was it really only seven?

In my experience, London games are rarely pleasurable. Being on the wrong side of six goal drubbings at Arsenal and Crystal Palace (for two consecutive seasons), conceding eleven at Chelsea in a matter of days in two different competitions, as well as a veritable potpourri of five, four, three, two and one goal defeats, leaves you, after a while, with a huge M25 shaped chip on the shoulder, while bemoaning natural Cockney talent. To this day, I understand that all Argyle signings are still required to tick the 'we shall never win in London' box of their contracts.

In addition, preparation for London games needs to be thorough:

Allowed fifteen hours travelling time? Check.

A to Z stored in the boot, so you can't possibly hope to get to it in time? Check.

When you do pull over to get out the A to Z, you find yourself in a red route bus lane in which anyone found stopping for any reason at all will go directly to Pentonville. No passing Go, no collection of £200? Check.

Confirmed that the page you need in the ever-elusive A to Z was ripped out the last time you drove to this 'hell hole' in order to remind yourself to never watch Argyle get beaten in London again? Check.

Made absolutely certain that the pub in which you are meeting is away-fan friendly, but is a thirteen-hour Tube ride from the ground? Check.

Made the maximum possible cash machine withdrawals over the previous three days to sustain four hours in the capital? Check.

Great, we're off to Griffin Park. Which corner of the ground is the meeting pub in again? Of all the London grounds, Griffin Park is the most welcoming, both on and off the pitch. On this day, the air was electric.

With five pints of freshly squeezed premium lager berries safely onboard, myself and my travelling companions for the day, Gary Pollock, session drinker and heavy drummer (that may be the wrong way around), and Statto Kev, rolled into the away end. It was packed. It was noisy. It smelt – Pac-a-Mac in a light drizzle jus with seasonal foppy mid-nineties 'curtained' hair.

Despite the nose pollution, the singing started. We were confident and the omens were good. Two consecutive blanks from the games prior to this one, a stunning first game of the season 5-1 home defeat to that day's opponents and Peter Swan in defence – to blindly optimistic Argyle fans, this could mean only one thing, things could not get any worse, right? (It was only in the 1979/80 season that I'd discovered we weren't actually called Argyle Nil) What could possibly go wrong?

Well, we weren't just bad that day, we were truly dreadful. The goals seemed to fly in at regular intervals throughout the game – there wasn't a dull moment. Headers, volleys, right foot, left foot, penalties, own goals – they all flew in from every possible angle.

Brentford 7

Argyle 0

BRENTFORD FOOTBALL CLUB

PASS OUT D BLOCK

MATCH

17 DEC 1994

DATE

Above: For those who may have been tempted to leave before the end…

Right: Surprisingly, there were no odds offered for a 7-0 home win.

Losing 1-0 or 2-0 is a dry and miserable experience, but this was superbly comical. The long-suffering Argyle fans began to celebrate the Brentford goals. 'We want six' – granted. 'We want seven' – granted. 'We want eight' – denied, but probably only because the novelty of scoring had worn off by then.

The gallows humour emanating from one end of the ground that day was nothing short of hilarious. The resigned helplessness and shock created an almost euphoric acceptance that we were, as we had suspected for quite some time, absolutely and unequivocally bad. But it didn't matter, this was as much fun as you could have watching Argyle lose.

It is an often-used cliché to say 'we were lucky to get nil that day', but we were. Attacking down the left, and with the Brentford players probably still celebrating their last goal, an Argyle player suddenly found himself in space and on a loose ball on the edge of the box. With a deft touch, his lazy lob drifted over the Brentford keeper and the ball bounced towards the goal. It's going in, and it's hilarious, we are at least twenty-five goals down and we are going to score! Get ready lads, we are going to celebrate this one, here it comes, get ready, nearly there. It's bounced wide.

We were disappointed, but not as crestfallen as the player himself. He was crushed and I really don't know why. Surely he must have known that we had left it too late to come back from being seven down? Right then, where were we? 'We're so s—— it's unbelievable!'

Mark Cleeve

THE DEFEATS AT the hands of Brentford were amongst the low points in a season that saw the Greens concede 83 League goals and finish relegated in twenty-first place.

Argyle: Hodge, Patterson, Swan, Burnett, Evans, Crocker, Comyn, Barlow, Nugent, Dawe, Ross. Sub: Shilton.

Bury v. Argyle

Date: 2 September 1995
Location: Gigg Lane

Football League Division Three
Attendance: Attendance: 3,040

When the fixtures for the 1995/96 season were released, Bury away was one of the first games I looked for as Gigg Lane was one of the few grounds I hadn't visited. I was determined to get there that season, but after a nightmare start of six straight defeats (four in the League and two in the League Cup), things did not bode well for the trip to Bury, and indeed the season ahead.

With this in mind, it seemed like it was going to be a fruitless trip, especially given that the Gigg Lane outfit had not lost at home for 22 matches, stretching back more than twelve months. Normally, I travelled everywhere with the London branch, but for this particular game there was little interest, so no rail trip had been organised. I nearly didn't go, but the Mrs decided she would like to come along and watch the game, so we decided to drive up north from our London home.

The Argyle fans, who were very few in number, were given a seated area at the far end of the main stand. I can remember being impressed by the newly completed South Stand, which was the first part of a complete rebuild of the ground in the nineties. What struck me most was that all the Argyle fans around me had the same 'What the hell am I doing here?' expression on their faces.

Little did we know it at the time, but Neil Warnock had pulled off a masterstroke by making Bury old boy Ronnie Mauge skipper for the day. Obviously, Mauge got the inevitable taunts from the Gigg Lane fans, but he shrugged these off to orchestrate a scintillating Argyle team performance which ripped apart a good Bury side, who, ultimately, would finish above Argyle in third place and gain automatic promotion.

Argyle weathered the early pressure from Bury to gain complete control and launched their long-delayed quest for promotion to Division Two. It was skipper for the day Mauge who provided the pass that opened the floodgates. It had looked a lost cause as the ball sped towards the goal line, but Ronnie athletically hooked the ball back to Michael Evans, who slid in to put it over the line. Evans had been selected ahead of the goal-shy Kevin Nugent after being the eternal substitute.

Twelve minutes and several missed chances later and Gary Clayton was celebrating his glorious twenty-five-yard chip that had completely bamboozled the back-pedalling Bury keeper before dipping underneath the crossbar.

Argyle, now full of confidence, went all out for the kill and found it through the tireless Chris Billy. He lifted the ball into the roof of the net on the stroke of half-time after Littlejohn had nodded down a superb cross from Paul Williams. Williams had outpaced ex-Argyle defender Ryan Cross and survived a very crude challenge before picking out Littlejohn with a peach of a cross. I, along with the Argyle faithful, was stunned, and I spent half-time wondering if 3-0 was going to be enough, but I need not have worried about a Bury recovery.

The interval made little difference to the pattern of play and Ian Hughes getting his marching orders after a professional foul on Littlejohn didn't help Bury's cause. With the absence of Hughes, Argyle created more and more gaps, from which Evans and Littlejohn profited greatly.

Bury 0

Argyle 5

Evans (2), Clayton, Billy, Littlejohn

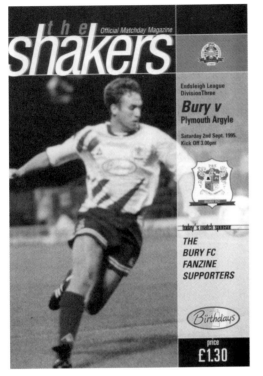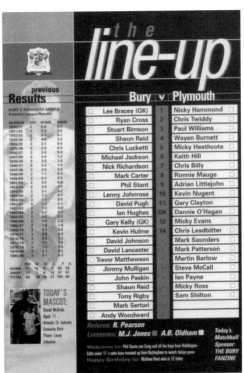

Above, left and right: The matchday programme (courtesy of Dave Pay).

Evans grabbed his second in the eightieth minute when he deftly flicked a thirty-yard chip over the stranded Bracey. Then, in the closing minutes, with Argyle completely dominant, Littlejohn out-stripped the tattered Bury defence and slotted home a quite superb fifth into the bottom right-hand corner of the net.

In the whole game, I cannot recall Kevin Blackwell being tested once, and the home fans showed their disgust by chanting for the manager's head, which with hindsight was a little premature given Bury's ultimately successful campaign. This result helped kick-start the 1995/96 season, which would end with a glorious play-off success at Wembley.

Kevin Buckthought

Argyle: Blackwell, Patterson, Williams, Clayton, Heathcote, Hodgson, Billy, Mauge (Saunders), Littlejohn (O'Hagan), Evans, Leadbitter.

Argyle v. Colchester United

Date: 15 May 1996

Location: Home Park

Football League Division Three play-off semi-final (second leg)

Attendance: 14,525

A beautiful and long day. I was working for the Immigration and Nationality Department at the infamous Lunar House and went in wearing an Argyle T-shirt. I received lots of patronising good wishes from workmates to little Plymouth from the bottom division. My protestations that this was the first season we'd ever spent there and that we wouldn't be going back fell on deaf ears.

Back home, oggy eaten and standing in my usual spot in the Devonport End, I never doubted we'd win. I'm not sure why, as I'm usually a pessimist and we were one goal down from the first leg on the previous Sunday.

There had been a bit of needle leading up to these games. The Colchester manager accused us of buying success whereas his team were the plucky, more skilful little guys. Bound to happen I suppose as, in truth, we were always a big fish in the bottom division pond.

The team didn't take long to show my confidence was not misplaced. Trigger powered a shot into the Devonport End goal early on and Chris Leadbitter got a second through a free-kick not long before half-time. Two excellent goals. Funny how some of Trig's best goals have been so important!

Great stuff, but the second half was when the atmosphere stepped up a gear and Home Park really started rocking. First, Mark Kinsella, who we later unsuccessfully tried to sign, scored an even better goal – a long-range cracker – and ran all the way to the bench to leap into his boss's arms. Cue biting of nails all around and Mr Warnock's famous sending off. Strangely, I was still confident.

Paul (Charlie) Williams, almost certainly the smallest man on the pitch, got on the end of a cross at the Barn Park End and that was always going to be it. His celebration is one of my favourite Argyle memories of all time. He was a quick little guy, but no one ever saw him as quick as we did at that moment. He wheeled away and raced back towards the Devonport. No one was going to catch him. Once in our half of the pitch, he threw himself to the ground and skidded along on his belly with his arms outstretched. Fantastic!

We were going to Wembley and if we had had to spend a solitary season in the bottom division to do it, maybe it was worth it. After all we wouldn't be going back, would we?

Kim Head

To use one of the beautiful game's most hackneyed clichés, football is a funny old game.

Two years before this infamous night, we had been beaten by Burnley, a team who finished three places below us. The accepted opinion was that the play-offs were a rip-off – a needless, end-of-season lottery that rewarded those teams who'd had a mediocre season, at the cost of those who had been fighting near the top throughout.

Still, nobody complained when we won that very same 'lottery'. It was, after all, our only chance to escape football's basement, which we had just sunk into for the first time. School couldn't have ended

Argyle 3	Colchester United 1
Evans, Leadbitter, Williams	

Neil Warnock rages from the stands.

We're on our way to Wembley!

PLYMOUTH ARGYLE FC
HOME PARK, PLYMOUTH PL2 3DQ
OFFICE: 01752 562561   PILGRIM LINE 0839 442270

T.B.A.	PLYMOUTH ARGYLE V
T.B.A.	THIRD DIVISION PLAY OFF
MAYFLOWER ENCLOSURE	MAYFLOWER ENCLOSURE
No. 1414	No. 1414

ADULT	ADULT	DATE TO BE ADVISED
£ 7.00	£ 7.00	**T.B.A. K.O.**
CONCESSIONARY	CONCESSIONARY	You are advised to take up you position half an hour before the kick-off.
£ 5.50	£ 5.50	This ticket is valid for the above match on whatever date it may be played.
TO BE GIVEN UP	TO BE RETAINED	Issued subject to the rules and regulations of the Football League and the Football Association.

quickly enough. After receiving no less than four warnings about not paying attention in class (fantasising about the various twists and turns that a football match can bring), I walked home to nervously consume dinner before being whisked off to the Civil Service Club at Beacon Park. That was where all the Argyle-supporting dockyarders (of which my father was one) convened before a match.

With the butterflies in my stomach already flying around with all the ferocity they could muster, I saw a man selling 'Argyle At Wembley 1996' T-shirts. This same man had sold similar T-shirts before the second leg against Burnley. 'Don't tempt fate', I whispered under my breath. Inside the stadium, vouchers were handed out, offering reduced-price tickets to the play-off final. By now, my patience was wearing thin.

Then to the game itself. Well, obviously the atmosphere was electric. The Colchester United fans were eventually to go home disappointed, which was just as well because they barely filled half the away end. The Devonport End was absolutely rocking, and even the old dears in the Mayflower seats managed to get one or two songs going – an indication, if one were needed, that this was to be a special night.

This game is already well documented, but I think a run-down of the highlights is worth another airing. Argyle started off kicking towards the Devonport, already 1-0 down from the first leg. Mickey Evans, who had already scored some breathtaking goals that season, scored what was – in my opinion at least – his very best. The ball came in and Trigger blasted it in from the edge of the area. Already, honours were even. It wasn't long before Chris Leadbitter scored from a free kick. 2-1 and three sides of the ground were going mental.

Colchester United, who included some future stars in their line-up, came back at us quite well in the second half, and one of those stars, Mark Kinsella, scored with a beautiful shot from outside the area. Not only a devastating blow but – horror of horrors – an away goal. Argyle led the game, but needed one more.

Matters weren't helped when our great leader Neil Warnock was sent away from the dugout by the referee. Nobody could quite tell what he'd done wrong, but we were all amused when he leapt over the fence into the Mayflower Stand and continued watching the game from there. Something I've not seen at a football game since.

Opposite and right: Ticket and programme from one of the most dramatic nights in Argyle's history.

I probably don't need to tell you that we got the goal we needed. Paul Williams scored it, and from then on it was just about holding on against a very tired and deflated Colchester side. The final whistle blew, and the rush of emotion from the Argyle fans was something I didn't see again until the QPR game in 2004. Thousands ran onto the pitch. We weren't promoted yet, but who cares? We were going to Wembley!

In the car on the way home (our legs far too jelly-like to walk), travel plans were made. My dad's friend (who owned the car, and coincidentally had family in Colchester) got out to talk to someone who, it transpired, owned a mini-bus. Getting back in the car, he exclaimed, with all the pride possible, 'That's the travel sorted! What plans have you got?' Rhythmic, unison beeping of horns followed as we waited to get out of the car park on what had been, at the time, the most amazing night of football I had ever seen at Home Park.

Andy Owen

Argyle: Cherry, Patterson, Williams, Mauge, Heathcote, Barlow, Leadbitter, Logan, Littlejohn, Evans, Curran

ARGYLE v. DARLINGTON

Date: 25 May 1996

Location: Wembley

Football League Division Three play-off final

Attendance: 43,431

This will be remembered as the most emotional day of my life. I had been to Home Park often that season with my granddad, who would take me down by train from Bristol. Shortly after the Colchester play-off game, he suffered a series of huge strokes which affected his way of life greatly. He had already bought the tickets to the final and got me a shirt with 'Play-Off Finalists' inscribed on the front and back. So when the day came around, it was left for my dad to take my brother and me by train from Gloucester to Wembley.

The train to Swindon was packed with Argyle fans and every carriage was decked out in green and white. On arrival at Swindon, where we had to board a train from the West Country, the number of Argyle fans was staggering. What really made me lost for words was that the trains that went straight through Swindon on their way to Paddington were jammed with Argyle fans. Each train was decked in flags, scarves and banners – even the driver's cabin was covered in Argyle colours.

On arrival in Paddington, you could see that the entire West Country had descended on London with the intent of making as much noise as possible and thoroughly enjoying their day out. Each tube to Wembley was crammed full and our carriage was no different. The entire train was in full voice singing, 'Now you've gotta believe it, the Greens are going up'.

I remember walking up Wembley Way without even seeing any Darlington fans, just a sea of green and white. As kick-off approached, the noise was incredible. I'd never witnessed a crowd of Argyle fans this large before and the hairs were standing up on the back of my neck.

The game itself was not brilliant, with both sides not wanting to lose. There was the occasional anxious moment from Darlington when the Green Army fell silent and the faint whispering of Darlo fans was to be heard. Midway through the second half, Wembley erupted, as the well-worked corner fell to the head of Ronnie Mauge. I went crazy, absolutely bonkers, as did my brother and even my dad, who was reluctant to come, being a Bristol City fan.

The last quarter of the game felt like the entire ninety minutes in one go. The scenes that followed the final whistle were incredible and unbelievable. The noise was louder than before and getting louder by the minute. My eyes were filling up more and more with thoughts of my granddad – he would have dearly loved to have been there after years of following Argyle. When the trophy was lifted, a roar which must have shook London followed.

The journey home was fantastic, train after train ran back to the West Country full of chanting fans overjoyed. Back at Swindon, everyone was on a high and whilst waiting for our connection, I remember a train pulling in and a woman running off to give me a big kiss and hug, then sprinting back to the train to carry on her journey. It was an unbelievable game, one of my favourite games ever watching the Pilgrims, just one thing was missing – my granddad.

Ryan Powell

Argyle 1
Mauge

Darlington 0

Above left: Neil Warnock and Mick Jones lift the trophy.

Above right: Mick Heathcote makes 35,000 Argyle fans very happy.

Ronnie Mauge and the team celebrate the winning goal.

ARGYLE v. DARLINGTON

This was the first time that I'd ever been to the hallowed turf. I had said to myself after being asked many times to go to the FA Cup final or a home international that I would only ever go to Wembley when Argyle played there.

The dream came true for me, albeit for a play-off final. I took in the atmosphere inside and outside the ground, seeing the Green Army all over the place. Those Twin Towers as we walked up Wembley Way were a sight to behold. Then, after getting inside the ground, my memories are of walking out into the seating area and seeing a mass of green and white. What an awesome sight! I remember just gazing around the stadium, absolutely gob-smacked and thinking 'My team are about to take to the pitch'.

The game was a bit of a blur and certainly tense – we had more to lose than Darlington. That was until the fateful moment! It was Argyle's first corner of the second half and the ball rolled back to Mark Patterson, whose cross was headed in by 'Da Gangsta' Mauge. I can remember being hugged and jumping around like a lunatic with total strangers.

Again the blur, was this happening for real? Then, the sheer emotion of the final whistle. I glanced up at the scoreboard and it read, 'Division Three Play-off Final Winners', and then, 'PLYMOUTH ARGYLE' in big lights. Then it sank in. I looked around and saw grown men sobbing with joy and heard the raptures of Queen's *We Are the Champions*.

It brought a lump to my throat, but boy did I sing it! The final thought on that wonderful day, when I looked over to the Darlington fans, was, 'What if that was us?' I felt sorry for them because it's a lottery when you look at it and it could so easily have been us. The journey home seemed to take minutes, but the memories will never fade!

Andy Laidlaw

I had already booked a holiday in Scotland, as I normally did when the season ended, so I had to travel down on my own from Edinburgh to meet friends in London. The missus didn't speak to me for a week as I had kept it secret from her, knowing she'd go ballistic. I wasn't wrong.

I remember getting on the train to go back to Scotland, wearing the shirt and a green wig, and walking into a carriage full of Darlo fans, who were all thankfully good natured. We all got 'mullered' together on the long trip home.

I have memories too, strangely, of anger – anger at having 5,000 gates, or less, for most of the season, only to have over 30,000 turn up at Wembley. Where were they every week? The Green Army chant, however, was awesome. The Greens on one side of the ground would mirror the other side. It still sends shivers down my spine thinking about it.

Wembley Way was awash with green flags, green scarves, wigs, and face-painted kids. You'd get a glimpse of some Darlo black and white once in a while, but we totally swamped them.

I knew the minute the ball hit Ronnie's head that it was going in, and kneecapped myself on the seat in front. Get in!

Leon Hannaford

I remember that bloke who turned up at every service station from Plymouth to Reading, selling his own brand of unofficial 'Argyle at Wembley 1996' scarves. Prices started at about £15 apiece at Home Park, and gradually decreased to about 50p by the time we got to Reading.

I also remember starting a chant off at Wembley (blushes with pride). The fat Darlington streaker and my

Left: The fans celebrate the Wembley win (photo courtesy of Nigel Springthorpe).

Below: Argyle finally get to Wembley.

mate Adam, not known for his great sense of vision, loudly berated an Argyle player they believed to have been a Darlo man who was down injured at the time, chanting, 'Cheat! She fell over…' Cue a barrage of pasties straight at his mush. Kelvin Noon RIP, you never got to see it, mate, and that breaks my heart.

Craig Stevens

We were on the M25 heading toward Wembley and Concorde flew over us as it ascended from Heathrow. My brother, not known for his one-liners, came out with 'that'll be us today – soaring high'. Of course, he was correct.

Paul Squire

Argyle: Cherry, Patterson, Williams, Mauge, Heathcote, Barlow, Leadbitter, Logan, Littlejohn, Evans, Curran

BURNLEY v. ARGYLE

Date: 2 May 1998
Location: Turf Moor

Football League Division Two
Attendance: 18,811

I remember boarding the supporters' coach at Home Park with a friend of mine, full of what turned out to be ill-placed optimism, dressed in Argyle colours, including a green wig and an oversized hat.

We set off for the journey to Turf Moor, confident that we could get the result that would keep us up. A packed away end greeted the boys in green and the atmosphere generated by both sets of fans was electric.

We were hoping Argyle would make a bright solid start and frustrate the home fans but, sadly, this did not happen, and Argyle conceded early on. Bravely, Argyle battled on and we got our just reward, with Mark Saunders rising to head the ball home to make it 1-1. The away end erupted and three quarters of Turf Moor fell silent. My heart filled with renewed hope – Argyle could stay up.

At this point, I did something that I had never done before and left during the match to go to the toilet. Just as I left the Grandstand, Turf Moor erupted once more. Sadly it was the Argyle fans who were now silent as we conceded what proved to be the decisive goal. Never have I left during a match since!

With results in other matches as they were, a point would have been good enough. I spent the rest of the match praying, wishing, hoping, believing, along with every other Argyle fan inside that ground, that Argyle would get the goal they needed. Sadly, it did not arrive and Argyle were relegated.

Grown men, including myself, cried like babies at the final whistle. I left the ground and boarded the coach to the jeers and taunts of the Burnley fans. We set off for the long, depressing journey home. It was a sombre and quiet atmosphere on the coach, broken only by the sound of rival fans car horns as they passed the coach, taunting us with our misfortune. It remains my worst day as an Argyle fan.

Justin Locke

This match was the last of a long season of travelling for the Cornish supporters. The 5a.m. start was nothing new for such an away trip in a season that saw the bus depart from Penzance at 3a.m. for the Carlisle away match and get back to the far West almost twenty-four hours later.

We travelled with optimism, despite the dire consequences of defeat as Mick Jones and his men had given us at least a chance of staying up. A draw was probably going to be enough as long as the Brentford result went our way. We arrived up north in good time after the customary supermarket breakfast in the Bristol area. Our then travel secretary Gary Curran came up trumps with a suitable hostelry in Darwen in which to take our pre-match refreshment. The locals wished us well, being in the Blackburn vicinity.

The incredible turnout of Argyle fans that day will be a lasting memory as we filled the outdated wooden seats of the away end at Turf Moor. The game summed up that season as Argyle gave everything and got nothing when the goal from Mark Saunders had given us so much hope. It was certainly a very emotional day, even without the amazing support and the significance of the game.

We had recently lost Noddy, one of the great Argyle characters, and I'd been to his funeral along with many fans, players and officials. The chants of 'Do it for Noddy' rang out all afternoon and no doubt

Burnley 2	Argyle 1
	Saunders

Left: A horrible moment for Paul Wotton.

Below: A black day for the Green Army as Argyle are relegated on the last day at Turf Moor.

he would have taken the result worse than most on that unforgettable afternoon in the North. The mindless Burnley fans that ignored the FA directives not to go on the pitch or face the non-existent consequences added to the gloom.

A friendly local wished us a safe journey home and I couldn't imagine what it might have been like if we'd done it that day and Earl Jean had connected with that cross near the end.

Chris Dennis

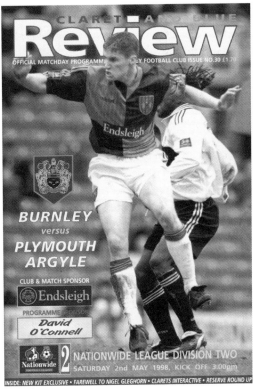

Argyle: Sheffield, Corazzin, Williams, Starbuck, Saunders, Currie, Woods, Heathcote, Conlon, Wotton, Barlow. Subs: Collins, Jean, Mauge

CARLISLE v. ARGYLE

Date: 8 May 1999

Location: Brunton Park

Football League Division Three

Attendance: 7,599

Two away games in the North in the final week of the season – not what Argyle would have chosen, especially since one or other of those two teams was going to be relegated to the Conference. On the Tuesday evening, Argyle had rolled over for Scarborough to put Carlisle at the bottom of the league. I just had to go to this one, partly because Argyle could never play worse and partly for the possibility of seeing a team that once topped the Football League falling out at the other end.

Carlisle is only a couple of hours from Huddersfield, so the drive up was pretty uneventful, as was the town itself. All the important action was going to be in the ground, so I got there in plenty of time.

The banter started before kick-off. There were a couple of hundred green shirts seated in the far end of the impressive stand that flanks one side of the ground giving it large to the Carlisle fans – letting them know that the Conference was a foregone conclusion and they might as well just get used to the idea.

Interestingly, we were separated from the rest of the Carlisle fans in the stand by a piece of flimsy netting that covered about four rows of seats. There weren't too many stewards around either. Some of us began to wonder what might happen to that little piece of netting if the banter got out of hand. Those concerns were raised a little more when Lee Phillips scored his one and only goal for Argyle to put us ahead early in the second half.

It was actually a pretty good goal and obviously quite important to Lee. He picked up the ball in the middle of the Carlisle half, managed to side step a tackle or two and then let fly from just outside the Carlisle area. For Argyle fans who weren't used to winning away from home, this was looking like a good trip – apart from the fact that Paul Gibbs had been carried off with a broken leg.

The Carlisle fans were getting restless by this stage. Scarborough were fighting for a draw at home to Peterborough, so the Blues had to win. We were never certain whether Michael Knighton was in the ground that day, but he was getting plenty of abuse in his absence. As time went by, the Argyle faithful reduced the banter levels.

There was a growing realisation that several thousand people in the ground were not very happy and we were obvious targets for any outpouring of emotion.

Tension was released when Carlisle equalised. Another good goal struck from distance; James Dungey just didn't seem to get a decent view of the shot. Cue a pitch invasion, resulting in several minutes' delay, that meant the Scarborough result was known before our match concluded.

As we passed the ninety-minute mark, the Carlisle fans knew they had to win. A couple of years later, I found out from a bunch of Carlisle supporters that they were ripping the seats out of the stands at that point and were planning to riot. Argyle fans sat in trepidation, some left early, whilst others were looking for stewards who might protect us. However, in the ninety-fourth minute Carlisle won a corner and, in desperation, up came goalkeeper Jimmy Glass.

The corner was taken and the header went in towards the goal. Dungey saved it, but the ball didn't travel very far. It was Jimmy Glass, the on-loan goalkeeper, who was there to side-foot home the goal

Carlisle 2	Argyle 1
	Phillips

Left: The Argyle defence step aside for the hero of the hour.

Below: A surreal experience for the Green Army, as one Jimmy Glass writes himself into football folklore.

that kept Carlisle in the League and relegated Scarborough.

After the ensuing pitch invasion, there was only time for Argyle to kick-off before the final whistle blew and there was another invasion. A good few Argyle fans stayed behind to applaud Carlisle on the greatest of great escapes and there was much handshaking and exchanging of shirts and scarves. Everyone left the ground that day thinking they had probably got off the hook.

Steve Barrie

ARGYLE'S BIT-PART role in Carlisle's 'Great Escape' was amongst the few remarkable moments of this dire season. The Greens ended the campaign below Exeter City in thirteenth place in Division Three – the lowest ever finish for Argyle.

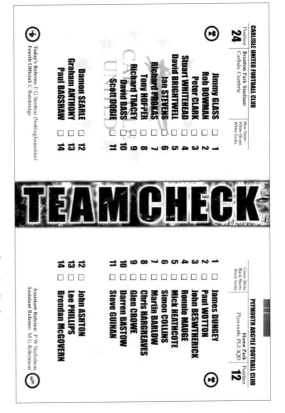

Argyle: Dungey, Collins, Crowe, Gibbs, Ashton, Guinan, Beswetherick, Heathcote, Phillips, McCall, Barlow. Subs: Wotton, Bastow, McGovern

Cheltenham Town v. Argyle

Date: 23 November 1999
Location: Whaddon Road

Football League Division Three
Attendance: 5,140

At the time, I was at school just outside of Cheltenham, so most friends either supported the Robins or loved teasing me about Argyle losing. When Cheltenham got promoted to the Football League and the fixtures for the season were announced, I couldn't wait for this night. Surely Argyle couldn't lose to an outfit that who, just a few years previously, had been playing in divisions below the Conference?

I had to beg my Dad to take me and, being a Bristol City fan, he was a bit reluctant. On the way, we picked up one of his work colleagues, a Cheltenham fan, and his son. As we approached the stadium, the Whaddon area was full of Argyle fans queuing for a ticket. I remember the police acting in a panic-stricken manner as thousands of the Green Army had descended on Whaddon Road, too many for Cheltenham's tiny away stand.

After much confusion, the police evacuated Cheltenham's C&G stand, meant for home supporters, and re-housed the Argyle fans. So, at kick-off, the number of Argyle fans must have come close to equalling the number of Cheltenham supporters. That was, and still is, my proudest moment as a member of the Green Army.

As the game got underway, the noise from the Argyle fans was deafening. Looking around, the faces of Cheltenham fans were of shock and disbelief that a team in Division Three could attract this many fans for an away game on a damp, cold Tuesday night in November.

Suddenly, Argyle hit self-destruct mode and conceded two goals, including a lob from just in front of the halfway line by Neil Grayson, a goal I'm reminded of by Cheltenham fans to this day. After the game, I couldn't help thinking what I was in for the next day at school, which turned out to be a torrent of abuse that kept coming until we beat them at Home Park. Martin Gritton, you are a saviour.

I thought Argyle had reached an all time low that night, but that was yet to come on Argyle's next visit to Whaddon Road.

Ryan Powell

What a day. We travelled up by minibus, arriving at about two o'clock. We parked behind the ground where there was a solitary steward. I asked him how many Argyle fans they were expecting. 'About 500' was his reply. I informed him that the estimate was a bit low. I walked away with him laughing at me.

We made our way to a pub called the Horse and Carriage, which slowly filled and by four o'clock it was heaving with green. At this stage, I got talking to the landlady. She had only taken over two weeks before and this was a Cheltenham home pub. By five o'clock, they had run out of draught beer and by six they had run out of bottles. Time to leave, as the first of the home fans arrived. It must have been a boring pub that night.

We eventually found the pub opposite the ground. It was surrounded by police, who had been drafted in from all over the area. Once inside, we realised why. It took twenty minutes just to get to the bar.

Cheltenham Town 2	Argyle 0

CHELTENHAM TOWN v. ARGYLE

The Green Army arrive in force, but Argyle are defeated by the Robins.

CHELTENHAM TOWN — PLYMOUTH ARGYLE

Manager: Steve Cotterill — Manager: Kevin Hodges

	Cheltenham Town	No	No	Plymouth Argyle	
☐	Steve BOOK	1	1	Jon SHEFFIELD	☐
☐	Michael DUFF	2	2	Jon ASHTON	☐
☐	Jamie VICTORY	3	3	Jon BESWETHERICK	☐
☐	Chris BANKS	4	4	Chris LEADBITTER	☐
☐	Mark FREEMAN	5	5	Mick HEATHCOTE	☐
☐	John BROUGH	6	6	Jason ROWBOTHAM	☐
☐	Lee HOWELLS	7	7	Martin BARLOW	☐
☐	Bob BLOOMER	8	8	Darren BASTOW	☐
☐	Neil GRAYSON	9	9	Sean McCARTHY	☐
☐	Dale WATKINS	10	10	Paul McGREGOR	☐
☐	Anthony GRIFFIN	11	11	Chris HARGREAVES	☐
☐	Shane HIGGS	12	12	Lee PHILLIPS	☐
☐	Hugh McAULEY	14	13	Steve McCALL	☐
☐	Richard WALKER	15	14	Paul GIBBS	☐
☐	Mark YATES	16	15	Paul WOTTON	☐
☐	Neil HOWARTH	17	16	Brendan McGOVERN	☐
☐	Russell MILTON	18	17	Liam FORD	☐
☐	Michael JACKSON	19	18	Adam BARRETT	☐
☐	Gareth HOPKINS	20	19	Kevin WILLS	☐
☐	Stuart MITCHINSON	21	20	Steve ADAMS	☐
☐	Steve BENBOW	22	23	Ian STONEBRIDGE	☐
☐	Martin DEVANEY	23	24	Wayne O'SULLIVAN	☐
☐	Nicky MARKER	25	25	Ken VEYSEY	☐
☐	Jason BRISSETT	26	26	Craig TAYLOR	☐
			27	Martin GRITTON	☐

The Green Army was now in full voice. Out came the landlord, who stood on a stool and announced to the 600 or so Greens that he didn't want us singing. That was like a red rag to a bull. All 600 seemed to start singing the same song in unison. At this point, the landlord made a hasty retreat back behind the bar and called the police. Six riot vans turned up, all because we were singing.

We made our way to the ground. The queue for the Argyle end stretched back as far as the eye could see. Only one thing for it – through the away end turnstiles, where the Cheltenham fans were now housed, and then a walk around the ground to join the gathering Greens. The game is best forgotten. On our way home, we passed the first pub. It was shut!

On a subsequent visit to Cheltenham, we went into the first pub and got talking to the same landlady. They had closed that night not only because they had no drinks, but they had also taken a week's takings in one night.

Warren (Wozzer) Bowden

IT WAS ANOTHER season in the doldrums for Argyle and they finished the campaign in mid-table, watched by crowds of just over 5,000.

Argyle: Sheffield, Stonebridge, Taylor, Leadbitter, Beswetherick, Barrett, McCall, O'Sullivan, Belgrave, Hargreaves, Heathcote. Subs: Bastow, McCarthy, Phillips

Rushden & Diamonds v. Argyle

Date: 27 August 2001

Location: Nene Park

Football League Division Three

Attendance: 4,414

'The start'. It's official, this game is now seen as the start of the rise of Plymouth Argyle. A hot balmy August Bank Holiday Monday in rural Northamptonshire for our first ever visit to Nene Park, home of the Doctor Martens-inspired Rushden & Diamonds. Paul Sturrock's first full season in charge had started strangely.

Bizarre defeats at home in the then semi-destroyed Home Park to Shrewsbury and Rochdale book-ended a spirited 0-0 draw at Boothferry Park against pre-season favourites Hull City and an excellent performance at Vicarage Road resulted in a 1-0 defeat to Watford, who at the time were two divisions above us. There was definitely potential in the new Paul Sturrock side, but he himself was quick to suggest that patience was the key and slow progress the aim.

Little did we know that day that we were about to witness not only the rare occurrence of an Argyle comeback away from home, but the game that really kicked off what would become one of the greatest seasons in the club's history. I wasn't initially planning to go, what with it being a Bank Holiday. Not being a driver, getting to Nene Park was nigh on impossible by public transport, so I was pleasantly surprised to get a phone call from Jerry Burnham, my Midland Green cohort and 'chauffeur', saying that he was going to drive over. So, off we went, meeting up with the usual away crew in a pub, which I think was called the Dragon, a couple of miles away from Irthlingborough, the spot in the middle of bloody nowhere where Max Griggs – owner of R&D and Doc Martens – had built his mini empire.

On arriving at Nene Park, where the locals were generally friendly, yet completely oblivious to the fact that the Division Three Champions for that season had arrived in their quiet corner of Northamptonshire, we were treated to a Tyhee Slim tirade in the queue to get in: 'It's like bloody Legoland, this'. But the one good thing about most Legoland-like stadia is that they all come with bars built in under the stands, and the crush to get served was reminiscent of the outdoor decks on the Titanic. More of that later (the bar, not the Titanic).

After a couple of cold ones watching Sky in the forecourt under the stand, commenting, 'Hope they put this in the New Dem'port and Lyndhurst', we took our very plastic seats in the very plastic stand. At least the view was a good one, and the Green Army was, as they were every single time that season away from home, in excellent voice.

Due to injuries and a couple of suspensions, the Argyle midfield had to be one of the youngest ever fielded, with both Joe Broad and Kevin Wills on the park. Argyle started badly, and Rushden controlled the game pretty much from the start, with Duane Darby, the ex-Torquay striker, causing problems for Wotton and Coughlan. Quickly enough, the inevitable happened and we were one down. Soon after, two down and it seemed like another miserable away trip was in the offing.

With five minutes to go, having watched another seemingly relentless Rushden attack, I decided that I'd had enough and announced to Jerry that I'd go and queue up to get a couple of beers in for half-time.

Joining a small band of fellow Greens who clearly had the same idea and were feeling as bloody

---

Rushden & Diamonds 2

Argyle 3

Evans, Coughlan, McGlinchey

Brian McGlinchey wins the game for Argyle.

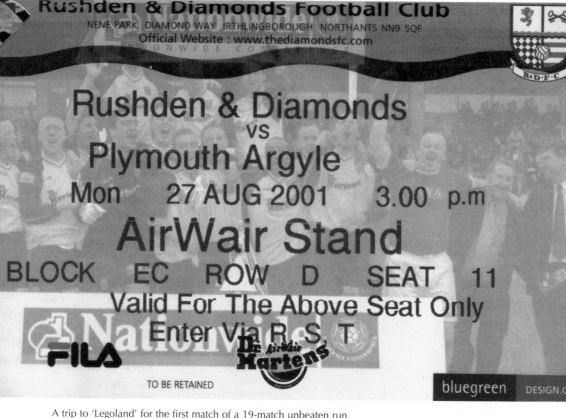

A trip to 'Legoland' for the first match of a 19-match unbeaten run.

miserable as I was, we proceeded to be thoroughly miserable together until, with the announcement of a couple of minutes of stoppage time, the Green Army gave a big roar. 2-1 – Trigger. Feeling a mixture of delight that we'd got one back and disappointment that I'd missed it, the goal and subsequent half-time whistle had brought a bit of needed cheer back to the Green Army, many of whom felt we could well nick a point now.

Second half kick-off, and it's all Argyle initially. Clearly Luggy's given them the soon-to-be legendary half-time 'Sturrock treatment', where he's used their heads to wipe the walls with and now they're playing like titans. Then comes the equaliser – Coughlan, from a Wotton corner. Rushden are still dangerous, and Romain continues to have an outstanding game and keep us in it.

Then comes the third, which I can remember very little about. I can recall it somehow falling to Brian McGlinchey on the outside of the box and it going in off the post. I may have dreamt it, but I'm sure he hit it with his unfamiliar right boot.

More Rushden pressure and jubilation from the Green Army at what was to become our first win of the season. And that was that. We laughed pretty much all the way back to Brum, at coming back from two down and from being bombarded for all bar the first twenty minutes of the second half.

Looking back now, to me that game changed everything. It was the first indication of the change in attitude at the club. Buoyed by what was a surprise victory, given the first half, Argyle went on an amazing run to the top of the table, passing Luton into first place at the beginning of October. We would lose top spot only once more for four days in April on our way to the Division Three Championship and a record points haul. But it was that day trip to 'Legoland' at the end of August that launched us on the way.

John Shattock

The inspirational Graham Coughlan celebrates with Brian McGlinchey at full-time.

Argyle: Larrieu, Adams, Coughlan, Wotton, Beswetherick, Phillips, Wills, Broad, McGlinchey, Hodges, Evans (Gritton).

Exeter City v. Argyle

Date: 18 September 2001

Location: St James' Park

Football League Division Three

Attendance: 5,756

What a day! As an art student at the time, I didn't have to take time out of work to make it on time. In fact, I probably had to get up a bit early for the 7.45p.m. kick-off, but it was worth it!

Travelling with two friends, we parked up in Exeter city centre. We'd been to the same fixture the previous season, a 2-0 win with one David Friio making an unexpected debut. An evening kick-off gave this fixture a different feel, with more anticipation probably. Fans were streaming towards St James' Park, police officers and their dogs lined the streets – a sad, but necessary part of the local derby atmosphere. As we queued along the residential road next to the away supporters' entrance, the Argyle fans were in good voice as ever.

Unfortunately, one of my friends had forgotten to remove his leatherman utility knife from his belt and the security conscious stewards confiscated it, for obvious reasons. He was told to come and reclaim it from the office after the game. Great. That would put an end to any plans we had of escaping any potential trouble! Still, on with the game – nothing we could do about it now.

And what a game it turned out to be. Argyle started well and it wasn't long before they took the lead. As irony would have things, it was Martin Phillips, the man who City sold years ago – and in doing so probably contributed to the club's financial survival – that scored with a close range drive. The Green Army were crammed in and that small away end shook with celebration!

Sadly, things then took a turn for the worse. As a former Exeter man had opened the scoring for Argyle, it was perhaps on the cards that the favour would be returned. Captain Chris Curran, formerly with Argyle and Torquay, equalised soon afterwards with a header.

If it seemed bad then, it was soon to get worse. Jon Beswetherick was having a 'mare at left back and, in attempting to let the ball run out for a goal kick, he was robbed by Christian Roberts and Argyle found themselves 2-1 down.

Paul Sturrock's team were deflated and were allowing their rivals to dominate the game. This continued after half-time as Argyle struggled to make any meaningful contribution to the game, but somehow they were thrown a lifeline when Mickey Evans headed past Exeter's on-loan keeper, Gregg.

Instead of wheeling away to celebrate, Trigger just stood with his head down, leading to a moment of disappointment where we assumed the referee had spotted an infringement. This feeling was soon followed by relief, however, as we realised Trig was probably just knackered!

Many of us would probably have settled for 2-2 by this point, to be honest. The performance had not been good and, had it gone the other way, I think we'd have felt robbed. But if Exeter had been robbed by Trigger's equaliser, I can only imagine what they thought when Ian Stonebridge popped up with a fantastic headed winner in the last minute! Unlike Mickey, Stoney celebrated straight away, and so did the ecstatic, grateful Green Army. All the way home.

Exeter City 2

Argyle 3

Phillips, Evans, Stonebridge

Above: Buster celebrates with the Green Army.

Right: A memorable night at St James' Park for the Green Army. Note that the ticket suggests that the Argyle fans should take their seat thirty minutes before kick-off – on a terrace!

Not for us though! Still shell-shocked, we made the slightly intimidating trek into the club office under the Old Grandstand, through hordes of Exeter fans with faces as green as our shirts, to pick up Steve's Leatherman! Not an evening that I'll forget too soon!

Owen Jones

Argyle: Larrieu, Worrell, Beswetherick (Hodges), Coughlan, Wotton, Adams, Phillips, McGlinchey, Friio, Evans, Banger (Stonebridge)

ARGYLE v. LUTON TOWN

Date: 29 September 2001

Location: Home Park

Football League Division Three

Attendance: 5,782

Nearly 6,000 supporters crammed into the one open side of Home Park for a cracking game that became even more important with hindsight. Luton were top and fancied their chances against all-comers. Mouthy boss Joe Kinnear was happy to let everyone know it. Of course, this only served to motivate the opposition. Plus Plymouth were unbeaten in seven games.

Luton took the upper hand early on, running the midfield as Friio and Adams did little more than a spoiling job, with Argyle content to play on the break. Bent and Worrell were doubling up on danger man Valois. Up front, Luton had Steve Howard, a lumbering Herman Munster of a target man from the old school, and his predictably small side-kick, Dean Crowe, who had made a single loan appearance for Argyle earlier that season.

Luton took the lead after fifteen minutes from a simple corner routine. Valois swung the ball in, Larrieu parried a Howard header, and Crowe stabbed in the rebound. But the star of the match at this point was referee Andy Hall.

Home Park has witnessed some poor refereeing over the years and this was right up there. Virtually every tackle in the first half earned a booking. Physical contact was barely allowed. No advantage was played. The referee didn't favour one side, he simply had no idea what he was doing. Six players were booked in the first thirty minutes and there were no bad tackles.

Argyle equalised on twenty-one minutes. Stonebridge broke from just inside the Luton half and weaved his way to the edge of the area, before slipping the ball to his left for Phillips, who slammed a low shot past two covering defenders.

Five minutes later, Valois curled a free-kick onto the underside of the bar. Bent repaid in kind when his cross-shot hit the post for Argyle.

Meanwhile, Hall continued to dominate proceedings as free kicks and stoppages littered the match and I was cautioned for foul and abusive language. The high point of this idiocy came with the sending off of Michael Evans after thirty-seven minutes. Evans went up for a high ball with Coyne and allegedly caught him with his elbow. There were no appeals from either side. The puffed up official stopped play and sent Evans off. As Trigger walked off, he smiled in disbelief and said to the bench 'I didn't do anything'.

The injustice merely served to galvanise the Argyle spirit. It lifted the crowd and generated one of the noisiest afternoons I have heard on the Mayflower Terrace. Luton captain Nicholls and the Argyle bench were involved in some silliness, culminating in Nicholls pushing Argyle physio Paul Maxwell. There were attacks and chances at both ends.

Then from a corner right on half-time, and against the odds, Argyle took the lead. A near post effort from Wotton was nodded in by Friio in a textbook training ground manoeuvre. You wondered whether Plymouth would hold out in the face of an inevitable Luton onslaught in the second half. The referee

Argyle 2	Luton Town 1
Phillips, Friio	

Buster scores as Argyle come from behind to beat Joe Kinnear's Luton team.

certainly changed his tune, being reluctant to stop play at all, and only making two bookings when he had no choice. The drugs must have started to wear off.

Howard missed the first chance of the second period, allowing Larrieu to make a spectacular recovery save. A Wotton free kick sent the outside of the net bulging midway through the half. Howard fluffed another headed chance for Luton, while Stonebridge pushed a good opportunity wide. Luton's left-back, Taylor, had a rasping drive saved low to his right by Larrieu and Lee Hodges came close for Argyle in the late stages. Luton still had most of the possession, but Plymouth kept their shape and as the half wore on, Luton simply ran out of ideas. They were reduced to long-range pot shots into the construction site at the Barn Park End. The substitution of an ineffective Valois was the prime example of their frustration.

At the death, when the board showed five minutes of added time, the referee played eight. My abiding memory of the afternoon is the sight of Friio geeing up the crowd in the last minutes of the match and the whole Mayflower side responding. Terrific stuff.

Toby Jones

Argyle: Larrieu, Worrell, Wotton, Coughlan, Adams, Phillips (Hodges), Bent (Wills), Friio, McGlinchey, Evans, Stonebridge (Hodges)

ARGYLE v. EXETER CITY

Date: 26 February 2002

Location: Home Park

Football League Division Three

Attendance: 16,369

Sixteen thousand witnessed Argyle take on their Devon rivals, Exeter City, and not one left Home Park dissatisfied. Paul Sturrock put in Marino Keith to replace the injured Mickey Evans and after the game he probably had a quiet chuckle that his hand had been forced in this way.

Argyle moved forward from the start and their early pressure was soon rewarded. Excellent work by Ian Stonebridge ended with him playing the ball back, via Lee Hodges, to Jon Beswetherick, who crossed into Exeter's six-yard box. Goalkeeper Stuart Fraser missed the cross and, following a scramble involving Marino Keith and Steve Adams, Adams poked the ball home.

Argyle continued to dominate with Stonebridge prominent, ably assisted by Keith and Martin Phillips. On nine minutes, Phillips crossed from the by-line but Stonebridge's first-time shot was saved by Fraser amidst a crowd of players. Minutes later, the referee's assistant on the Lyndhurst side walked groggily across the pitch to be replaced by the fourth official and a bizarre refereeing decision saw Argyle awarded a corner on the right after a Paul Wotton free-kick was clearly deflected out on the other side.

Exeter started to gain more possession and Christian Roberts shot over from outside the Argyle area. A break from Phillips then saw David Worrell cross low, but Stonebridge could only head straight into Fraser's arms.

Then, from another free-kick after a foul by Chris Curran on Stonebridge, Beswetherick swung an excellent cross into a crowd of players and Keith managed to get his head to the ball to give Fraser no chance from close range. The crowd was then entertained by a streaker, naked but for a pair of shiny trainers (the only thing I noticed about him), who ran onto the pitch at the Devonport End. He got one of the biggest cheers of the night as he dived back into the crowd in an unsuccessful attempt to evade the stewards.

In the midst of some strong Exeter pressure, the referee proved that he expected to be listened to, awarding an Argyle throw-in to Exeter after Beswetherick failed to comply with his indication of where the throw should be taken. He promptly gave it back to Argyle when the Exeter player threw the ball in from the same position. A clash of heads between Graham Coughlan and Breslin saw physios racing onto the pitch, but in the end both players, though battered and bruised, were fit to continue.

With twenty minutes to go, Cornforth replaced Steve Flack with Sean McCarthy to howls of derision from the home crowd. McCarthy was soon in action, shooting well wide from long range. Prior to this, Lee Hodges almost scored a wonder goal with a left-foot volley that was pushed around the post by Fraser at full stretch. Argyle's third goal came on seventy-two minutes. Stonebridge broke through the Exeter defence, but was smothered as he approached the penalty area. The ball fell to Keith, on the edge of the penalty area, who picked his spot and curled an exquisite shot past Fraser into the corner of the goal.

The excitement was too much for one Argyle fan who ran onto the pitch, grabbed a corner flag and left a trail of stewards floundering in his wake before tumbling over and being escorted away.

Argyle 3

Adams, Keith (2)

Exeter City 0

Steve Adams begins the scoring as the Grecians are shot down at Home Park.

The excitement was also too much for Sean McCarthy who, after the re-start, saw red mist, smashed an elbow into Coughlan's face and promptly received his marching orders. Cornforth replaced Cronin with Paul Buckle, and Sturrock replaced Stonebridge, Phillips and Hodges with Blair Sturrock, Neil Heaney and Kevin Wills. In stoppage time, Wills was unlucky not to increase Argyle's tally when his low thirty-yard drive cannoned off the base of the post.

Paul Sturrock refused to talk about promotion, but most Argyle fans had little doubt about the ultimate success of their team. The whole side was on form, and with some bizarre refereeing, a streaker, the flag-waving fan and the fall of Sean McCarthy, the game had everything (including Mexican waves).

Tim O'Hare

Argyle: Larrieu, Adams, Beswetherick, Coughlan, Worrell, Wotton, Friio, Phillips (Heaney), Hodges (Wills), Keith, Stonebridge (Sturrock)

ROCHDALE v. ARGYLE

Date: 26 March 2002
Location: Spotland

Football League Division Three
Attendance: 4,457

Following the victory at Lincoln the previous Saturday, just a point was needed at Rochdale to ensure that Argyle were the first team to be promoted in England that season. For me, having witnessed our previous three promotions going back to 1974/75, it called for some hasty action.

After some hectic negotiations at work and home, by noon I was ready to set off for Spotland with fellow Sussex Green and lifetime supporter, Mike. My position was mirrored by hundreds of others, who suddenly found work commitments in the north or took holidays at short notice.

After a long and tortuous drive, we arrived at the rather morbidly named Cemetery pub at about six o'clock to meet up with two other Greens, Ian and Paul. Already thronging with the Green Army in good voice, this had all the hallmarks of a special night.

We were allocated a new stand along one side of the pitch in a tight but neat ground, helping fuel a highly charged atmosphere from the start. The guys with the inflatable champagne bottles set the tone, but Rochdale themselves had play-off ambitions and would not roll over. They had won at Home Park early in the season and doubtless recalled that we had cost them a play-off place by forcing a goalless draw in the final match of the season just under a year before.

The first sixty minutes of the game gave us few grounds for optimism. Rochdale attacked incessantly, with only Romain Larrieu keeping us in the game. Eventually, the pressure told, with a forty-yard screamer from Simpson into the top corner, which I still rate as the best goal I have ever seen.

Never one not to respond to the situation, Paul Sturrock was prompted to make a triple substitution, bringing on Marino Keith, Neil Heaney and Ian Stonebridge to provide some attacking depth. This brought instant reward, with Keith bundling the ball in after the Rochdale keeper, Gilks, dropped a Paul Wotton free-kick.

Fifteen minutes later, we took the lead when Graham Coughlan poked home following a corner, and the victory was sealed by Hodges thumping the ball home after a break by David Friio. This prompted a fantastic celebration, with the players diving in front of the massed ranks of Argyle fans. A pitch invasion was inevitable, but I still recall the vain efforts of a sole steward trying to turn back the tide when the final whistle went.

With 1,000 of the Green Army now positioned in front of the Grandstand, the team came out to celebrate with champagne flying everywhere. After a post match debrief in the Cemetery, the drive home was less than welcome, and I must confess to being pretty dopey in work the next day (I arrived back at 5.30a.m. and had to go to a meeting in London for 8.30a.m.), but it was well worth it.

For me, this was possibly the best promotion I have witnessed, even surpassing the events to follow two years later. Why? Well because after years of mediocrity and the despair of belonging in the basement division, there was genuine cause for celebration and hope for the future. It was also the first promotion achieved on an away ground in my lifetime (I exclude the Wembley play-off win as that was neutral).

Given the strength and commitment of our travelling support, this somehow seemed to be just reward for some long, and usually fruitless, hours on the road.

Rochdale 1

Argyle 3
Keith, Coughlan, Hodges

Marino scores as Argyle win promotion from Division Three.

And lastly, but not least, because of the warmth from the Dale supporters I spoke to who seemed genuinely pleased for us, even now, I look out for their results. As Mike put it, how is it that people living so close to Burnley are so different?

Roger Ball

Argyle: Larrieu, Adams (Heaney), Beswetherick, Coughlan, Worrell, Wotton, Bent, Friio, Sturrock (Keith), Evans (Stonebridge), Hodges.

CARLISLE v. ARGYLE

Date: 13 April 2002
Location: Brunton Park

Football League Division Three
Attendance: 3,080

Surreal is the only word to describe the trip to Carlisle, our penultimate away game of the 2001/02 championship season. Even though we had been promoted for almost three weeks, since the Rochdale game, nerves and tension were in abundance on the long trip up to Cumbria.

We'd just lost top spot to Luton on the preceding Tuesday after they had played a rearranged game and, even though we now had a game in hand at Darlington, it had been a frustrating week. We had been top for so long, and with the intense rivalry that had grown with Luton, the last thing we wanted to do was concede our title, particularly to them.

On top of that, all week the internet-based supporters had been contacted by Carlisle fans who, with it being their last home game of the season, were holding a protest and a picket against Michael Knighton, their barmy and despised chairman. A suggestion to us that we travel all the way up to Cumbria (many travelling from Plymouth) and then join them outside while our boys try and keep on the Championship trail was met with derision, but the general consensus was that whilst we were there to support the Greens, we would support the Carlisle fans in their protest also.

The journey up was long and uneventful and, as always, I felt a fraud for starting from Birmingham (what am I supposed to do, travel down to Plymouth the night before and then get the train all the way up?).

I had a few beers in a couple of pubs on Botchergate, and some friendly banter with the locals. I've done the trip to Carlisle before, and have always found them to be very friendly. I always got the feeling that there was a certain amount of kinship between us as we're both on the extremities of England. Well that and Jimmy Glass anyway! The fact that we were also making the right noises regarding their anti-Knighton protest made for a great atmosphere.

Up to Brunton Park and the picket and demo against Knighton, which we loudly applauded before going into the ground for a bizarre setting. We had brought, as usual that season, a large number of Greens – anything between 1,500 and 2,000. Many were staying up north for the weekend and going straight to Darlington for Monday, so with the large contingent of Greens, and hardly any Carlisle fans, as most of them were marching round the ground all afternoon, we were in a clear and very vocal majority.

This had no bearing on the boys, however, who, according to Paul Sturrock's Championship Diary, required no extra motivation or team talk. The look of sheer determination on Wottsie's face when he came out said it all, and you could almost hear the war cry emanating from the huddle. The game was total Argyle and was the most disciplined, clinical performance that I can remember.

The celebrations at the end heated up sufficiently when the shock result from Kenilworth Road came through. Luton had somehow managed to draw at home with Macclesfield. What that meant was that not only were we rightfully back on top of the table, but a win at Darlington two days later would crown us as Champions. We were almost there.

John Shattock

Carlisle 0

Argyle 2
Keith, Wotton

Marino starts the scoring.

This was the game where Argyle unveiled the Tangerine strip. I can still remember the incredulity which greeted the team when they trotted out. The Green Army was bolstered by a number of Dundee United fans, paying homage to Paul Sturrock, who certainly added to the atmosphere. They also gave us false hopes on the Luton versus Macclesfield result by cheering loudly on the basis of two 'radio' goals, which turned out to be north rather than south of the border. But we forgave them. There was a typical Cocko response at the end – charging across the pitch to us to find out how Luton had fared, punching the air with delight when he heard they had only drawn.

Favourite chant? 'You should be outside' to the few Carlisle fans inside the ground whilst the anti-Knighton brigade were making their numerous circuits around Brunton Park.

Roger Ball

Two things struck me about this day. Firstly, the Green Army was swelled by a number of Dundee United fans who had travelled across the border to support Argyle and the great god Luggy, wearing their club colours of orange. The Argyle team wore the new away strip of orange shirts and green shorts – you couldn't mistake them.

Secondly, there was a Carlisle supporter protesting at their board, trying to hold his banner up over the wall behind one of the goals. Every time he got up, he fell back. His protest fell on deaf ears. Who cared, another win, we were going up.

Malcolm Townrow

Argyle: Larrieu, Adams, Beswetherick, Coughlan, Worrell, Wotton, Bent, Evans, Hodges, Keith, Stonebridge.

DARLINGTON v. ARGYLE

Date: 15 April 2002
Location: Feethams

Football League Division Three
Attendance: 4,089

The day started at work. Ever since the victory at Carlisle United on the Saturday, I had been plotting how to explain to my boss, who was a non-football fan, that if we won this game we were champions. It was easier than I had anticipated. After a short explanation, his response was, 'Well, best you get off then!'

A few phone calls later and a rendezvous was arranged with others at the A1 services. The drive seemed short as we arrived in Darlo for our second visit of the season for the same game and, after a few 'warmers into the bank', we set off for the walk to the ground. On entering Feethams, I was greeted by a couple of blonde female twins. Well, the Brock boys made a number of the local girls look ugly.

The teams arrived, Argyle in their 'tangergreen' strip which shone under the floodlights. The atmosphere was fantastic, standing on the old terraces, with chants of, 'Sit down if you love the Greens'. It was clear from the start that our confidence, skill and style of play were going to allow us to see Argyle win their first championship trophy for many a year.

The goals were class – a brace from Marino Keith, and one apiece from Trigger and Jason Bent. Even when Darlington scored their goal, we knew that this was the night. With the end of the game near, we were all involved in friendly banter with the Darlo stewards, and they were firm but helpful in their handling of the Tangergreen Army. The final whistle blew and off we went onto the pitch.

I remember getting close to Romain and trying as nicely as I could to prise one of his gloves from his hand. He wasn't having it, although Trigger lost or gave his shirt to some lucky fellow. The team went, after what seemed an age, to the stand, and there were many chants including, 'Are you watching Joe Kinnear?' and 'Champions!'

The journey home was swift. Happy talk on a return from an away game was, up until this season, a rare occurrence. It was a night that will stay with me for ever, the image of the Green Army as one winning with such confidence on a happy night 'oop north'!

Colin Carr

A futile visit by the Leeds Greens to the original fixture ended in a blizzard the likes of which I'd only seen before in Scunthorpe. So rescheduled it was, coming off the back of that tangerine-clad victory at Carlisle which put us so, so close. I'd had one previous visit to Feethams as a kid with my Dad – all the way from Devon on a dilapidated pink Tally-Ho coach to see us clinch second place under Ciderman in the 1985/86 season, thanks to Hodges and Tynan. A pitch invasion ensued.

This time around, echoing Sturrock's post-match comments of knowing there was only going to be one winner from the moment he saw the players leave the changing room, I had a feeling. Argyle duly delivered and raced into a two-goal lead from a nonchalant Trigger effort and one from Marino. So complacent

Darlington 1

Argyle 4
Evans, Keith (2), Bent

Above left: Trigger wheels away in celebration as the championship is sealed.

Above right: The crowd goes wild at Feethams (photo courtesy of Stuart Caskey).

Left: The original fixture was delayed by a blizzard, but Argyle made the second trip worthwhile as the Third Division championship was won.

was my joy that I missed the third goal, Marino's second, as I was yapping to fellow Leeds Green Neil Carhart and was interrupted by his cry of 'Another!'

Darlo pulled one back with a penalty, but never threatened and it finished 4-1, thanks to Bent's strike after a flowing move. As the whistle blew, the stewards gathered but within minutes they left, knowing that they would not be able to stop the eager and exuberant Green Army from trampling all over the pitch. Then the whistle – a huge roar went up and onto the pitch we went as one. Watery eyes everywhere – 'part payment back for the last ten years' said fellow Leeds Green Paul Luxton.

I hugged strangers and they hugged me. I rang my Dad, who had been glued to Sparksy, and could hear the emotion in his voice. I did not know then that he would only be with me for another year, but am now eternally glad he was around to see a championship, as he was the one who turned me Green. I know he felt represented when I was at matches and that the future was safe. Arriving home, I found a welcome committee of my Pilgrim Pete cuddly toy holding a champion's trophy fashioned out of an eggcup and silver foil by my partner Cath. Heaven indeed and it wasn't all a dream when I awoke!

Andy Chapman

Argyle: Larrieu, Adams, Beswetherick, Coughlan, Worrell, Wotton, Bent, Evans (McGlinchey), Hodges (Sturrock), Keith, Stonebridge (Phillips).

ARGYLE v. CHELTENHAM TOWN

Date: 20 April 2002

Location: Home Park

Football League Division Three

Attendance: 18,517

At about 4.45p.m. on Saturday 20 April 2002 at Home Park, the 1,500 or so Cheltenham fans at the Barn Park End started to sing. They were drowning out the home support, which outnumbered them by a ratio of about twelve to one. There's nothing unusual in that in football grounds these days – small bands of travelling supporters, bonded by togetherness and often fuelled by alcohol, will regularly out-sing the massed home support.

The difference on this occasion was that the home fans were merely clearing their throats. Argyle were leading 2-0, and it had been obvious from very early on that there was no other possible outcome in this game but a home win. All that was left now was the countdown to the final whistle and the subsequent presentation of the Third Division trophy to the team.

Still, the home fans responded magnificently to the defiant chants of the Robins' fans and within seconds it seemed as though the whole ground was chanting 'Ar-gy-ull, Ar-gy-ull, Ar-gy-ull'. It was the loudest I'd heard a Home Park crowd for years. From my vantage point (in the Grandstand for a change) I could clearly see the faces of the Cheltenham fans and their only possible response to this outbreak of joyous singing from the Green Army was to sit down, stop singing, and resign themselves to the fact that it was our day. Even some of the players looked impressed by the sheer volume of noise.

The championship was won and the final challenge had been to break the 100-point barrier. Well, that was the case for most, but for me beating Cheltenham was something that meant a lot.

I think my real gripe with Cheltenham went back to the day when we were beaten 5-2 at Whaddon Road. In an era when Argyle suffered one embarrassing defeat after another, and when I'd often think that it couldn't get any worse (until I went to the next game), this took the biscuit. I remember seeing us lose 3-0 at Lincoln, when I let rip with a foul-mouthed, beer-fuelled tirade after the third goal went in, which even caused a couple of our players to look up at the stand. There was also the 3-0 defeat at Leyton Orient on Easter Monday, when masses of Argyle fans saw one of the most spineless performances ever and a Liverpool fan (a guest of a Green) behind me, impressed with our support, said, 'they don't deserve yooz lot'; the hammering at Shrewsbury during the petrol blockades; and a 4-1 mauling at Macclesfield. But that day at Cheltenham was, for me, the lowest of the low.

So, beating Cheltenham on that beautiful day in April was really special for me. We had to win to avoid the season ending in anti-climax, to pass the 100-point barrier (an awful joke at the time was 'What's the difference between Argyle and the Queen Mother?', with the answer being that Argyle actually made it to 102), and also because professionally the players owed it to Mansfield to at least try to win the game. There was a feeling that some of the players had been celebrating quite enthusiastically since clinching the championship and that maybe their performance would suffer. I know that my milkman in Mansfield was convinced that our gallant lads would all turn up with hangovers and that Cheltenham would have a cakewalk.

Argyle 2

Bent, Coughlan

Cheltenham Town 0

Paul Sturrock takes the applause from the Home Park faithful.

David Friio and the team wait to lift the trophy.

He needn't have worried. The lads gave a great performance, with the nerves settled as early as the fourth minute when Jason Bent cracked a shot into the corner of the net after some sweet build-up play. Twenty minutes later the player of the year, Graham Coughlan, scored a slightly comical goal, winning a footrace with Steve Book, the Cheltenham goalie, after the hapless keeper had failed to control the ball. Cheltenham had a few half-chances, but the best move of the game saw Michael Evans unlucky to hit the crossbar with a header that left Book stranded.

Cheltenham huffed and puffed a bit in the second half without really threatening and you knew the game was up for them when they withdrew the tiring Julian Alsop who, despite being awful, had looked their most likely threat. The game was won, and for me it was significant that our last game in this terrible division was against the team that, for me, represented the nadir of the entire history of Plymouth Argyle.

That brings me back to the start, the defiant singing of the Cheltenham fans that died in their throats almost as soon as it began. As much as I disliked Cheltenham, their fans were a credit to them that day. They never stopped singing, apart from that last five minutes when they knew the game was up and the news that Mansfield were winning had filtered through, and many of them stayed behind after the game to applaud the presentation of the championship trophy. They were as generous in defeat as the QPR fans would be two years later. They finished fourth in the table and were promoted via the play-offs – a just end to their season as the team finishing in the first place behind the automatics deserves to be promoted, not some shower who finish twelve points behind, but that's another story.

Neil Jenkins

THE GREENS FINISHED their amazing championship campaign with 102 points from 46 games, having gone on an unbeaten run of 19 games following the win at Rushden & Diamonds.

Argyle: Larrieu, Stonebridge, Bent, Keith, Wotton, Coughlan, Friio, Beswetherick, Hodges, Worrell, Adams. Subs: Evans, Sturrock.

Port Vale v. Argyle

Date: 18 October 2003

Location: Vale Park

Football League Division Two

Attendance: 5,786

With 10 goals scored in the previous 2 games, confidence was sky high at Home Park. Luggy said before the game that it would be difficult choosing the sixteen who would be selected for this match – he had taken seventeen professionals to choose from. The starting XI was the same that had disposed of Tranmere just seven days earlier and there was another impressive turn out from the Green Army (over 600), who were in an expectant mood.

The only downside to my day was that, despite leaving Cheltenham at noon in order to get to the PASALB meeting pub for a few ales, along with several others, I got caught up in the queues behind an accident that blocked the M6 motorway. It took just over forty-five minutes to get to the M5/M6 interchange, but then it took another three hours to get to the ground via Walsall and Cannock. I arrived at 3.45p.m., expecting to greet the half-time whistle. Luckily, I managed to park right outside the turnstiles and, after discovering from a steward that the game had been delayed fifteen minutes, I took my seat and found out that, although there had been a few chances, the score was still 0-0.

Vale Park hadn't been a happy hunting ground over the years but, within five minutes of my arrival, the proverbial floodgates had opened. David Worrell stole the ball and, after crossing dangerously into the box, a neat back-flick from Evans saw Marino Keith stab the ball home at the second attempt. A few minutes later, it was two – Evans this time providing the cross, which found an unmarked Friio with the easiest of headed opportunities.

I'd have been quite happy with that, given the nightmare journey I'd had, but no, Argyle continued to press and, following more good work by Evans, his pass found Steve Adams on the edge of the box, whose left footed strike easily beat Delaney in the Vale goal. 3-0 at half-time and I had managed to see all of them.

Now, it has to be said that it isn't unknown for the Greens to take their collective foot off the gas when leading by so comfortable a margin, but that thought was put to bed shortly after the break when Argyle were awarded a free-kick just outside the box, well inside Paul Wotton territory.

An interchange of short passes between Friio and Ian Stonebridge allowed Wotton to open the angle and his rasping drive left the keeper no chance as it went in off the post.

Cries of 'We can see you sneaking out' and 'Cheerio, cheerio, cheerio' rose from the massed Green and Tangerine Army along with 'We want six' and 'Can we play you every week?'. However, within five minutes, Vale had pulled a goal back – McPhee swivelling in the box and beating McCormick for the first time in over five hours of football.

Most of the remainder of the game was end-to-end stuff as Vale, with little now to play for, laid siege to the Argyle goal. The defence, however, stood firm and the introduction of Tony Capaldi with twenty-five minutes left brought a new dimension to Argyle's attack. Several times his crosses provided a stern test for the beleaguered Delaney.

Port Vale 1

Argyle 5

Keith, Friio (2), Adams, Wotton

David Friio celebrates the first goal with the scorer Marino Keith.

With fifteen minutes to go, the four-goal lead was restored – Friio bagging his second with a stunning strike from range which was placed into the top corner. It was yet another goal-of-the-season contender and even the home fans appeared to appreciate it – those who were still there, that is!

The only downside was that his celebration earned him an unnecessary booking. He was substituted soon after by Jason Bent, whose first touch was a header from the six-yard line that the keeper did well to hold on to. Chances came and went for both sides in the final ten minutes, but no more goals. It finished, probably much to Vale's relief, 5-1.

Ian Scott

Argyle: McCormick, Adams, (Aljofree) Coughlan, Worrell, Gilbert, Wotton, Norris, Friio (Bent), Evans, Keith (Capaldi), Stonebridge.

SHEFFIELD WEDNESDAY v. ARGYLE

Date: 22 October 2003   Football League Division Two
Location: Hillsborough   **Attendance:** 20,090

There are not many things in life that would give you cause to crack open a bottle of champagne at 2a.m. on a work night, but that's just what Alastair McCulloch and I did after driving back from the scene of one of Argyle's greatest displays in a highly successful era.

Beating Sheffield Wednesday 3-1 on their own patch sent Argyle to the top of Division Two and announced our arrival as a club with serious intentions. True, that season was a lazy Sunday for Wednesday, but at that stage in the season (sixteen games in) they were still hovering around the top ten and most pundits were waiting for them to begin their march to the title.

But they were well and truly flattened by a cavalry in green as little old Argyle began a march to glory of their own on that most memorable of nights. The Pilgrims were riding the crest of a wave having just beaten Tranmere 6-0, Bristol City 4-0 and Port Vale 5-1, though any Argyle fans harbouring doubts in our ability to repeat the trick in the imposing surrounds of Hillsborough could have been forgiven.

It was by far the largest and most prestigious ground Argyle had visited for a League match since drawing at Newcastle more than twelve years previously.

Paul Sturrock's Pilgrims – blood, snotters and all – didn't stand on ceremony for even a moment, and after spending the first twenty minutes working out where Wednesday's weaknesses were, they duly exploited one when David Friio rose like a salmon from the Seine to dispatch the opener and send the already-raucous Green Army into raptures. The chant of 'Arrrr-gy-le, Arrrr-gy-le' rang out into the Yorkshire night as the home fans fell silent. The singing continued into half-time, and by the hour-mark had risen to a deafening crescendo.

Argyle quite simply destroyed Wednesday during a ten-minute period in which they scored twice more – a Paul Wotton penalty after David Norris had been tripped, and an even better header than his first from the incomparable Friio. My only regret about actually being there was not being able to hear Jeff Stelling bark out to Sky Sports viewers: 'Free-scoring Plymouth are doing it again tonight. David Friio has just put them 3-0 up at Hillsborough, and that's their eighteenth goal in four games! Unbelievable.'

Wednesday tried to out-Argyle Argyle in the closing stages, but their constant pummelling of our penalty area was schoolboy stuff and only resulted in one meaningless goal.

The home boos which greeted the full-time whistle were blown clean out of the stadium by the most rousing rendition of 'Arrrr-gy-le, Arrrr-gy-le', you are ever likely to hear. Our heroes had announced their arrival to the country, and we were just making sure they had been heard loud and clear.

Paul Roberts

3-1 at Hillsborough. I wouldn't have thought that possible when we were losing to Cheltenham at Whaddon Road a couple of years previously. To top the night off, we overtook the team bus on the M5, with the team all smiles, cheering with us and the bus driver flashing his lights and beeping his horn;

Sheffield Wednesday 1   **Argyle 3**
                                             Friio (2), Wotton (p)

A typically thunderous penalty from Paul Wotton seals a thumping win for the Pilgrims.

just us and the coach on an empty stretch of motorway. What a night, just what was needed to quiet the, 'Argyle are no good' brigade.

Ryan Powell

This was Hillsborough and this was my team about to go top of the League. When Friio's header sent the away end into total pandemonium and disbelief, at that moment I turned and celebrated with my dad. The look on his face said it all and will live with me forever. I gave him a big hug as we sang, 'We are top of the League' together. Whilst the Wednesday fans headed home, the loudest cheer was saved for the final whistle as we went top of the League in style. For everyone that went to Hillsborough that evening, it was a night they will never forget.

I didn't know it at the time, but this was to be my Dad's last full season supporting the Greens before his death. I went to hundreds of football matches with my Dad, but that night at Hillsborough and the moment when Friio scored the third goal will live with me forever. Thanks for the memories, Argyle. Thanks for the memories, Dad.

Steve Riggs

Argyle: McCormick, Adams, Gilbert, Worrell, Wotton, Friio (Bent), Norris, Evans, Keith, Stonebridge (Capaldi).

Swindon Town v. Argyle

Date: 13 December 2003

Location: County Ground

Football League Division Two

Attendance: 9,374

This is without a doubt the best away game that I have ever attended. Only on the Friday before the game did I find out that I would be able to go, as a mate of mine had a spare ticket and had offered me a lift. During Argyle's Division Two Championship season I decided that I would aim to attend at least half of the away games, with this being my first. There was a great turnout from the Argyle fans for what turned out to be a really eventful match.

After only fourteen minutes, Tony Capaldi broke through the Swindon defence to latch onto a long pass from Paul Connolly and side-foot home to make the score 1-0. We had to wait until the seventy-fifth minute before we saw another goal. David Norris was the scorer, making it 2-0 with a simple finish from only ten yards out.

This spurred a pretty dismal Swindon team into action. From what must have been one of their first corners of the game, the ball was scrambled home by Rory Fallon to give Swindon a glimmer of hope after eighty minutes. Surely not? Surely it was too late?

Then with ninety-one minutes on the clock, a long free-kick by Swindon defender Andy Gurney was once again scrambled home, this time by Sam Parkin. It was now 2-2, and there was surely no time left. At this point, every Argyle fan at the game, or listening on the radio, was absolutely gutted!

Then, just seconds after the restart, Swindon were reduced to ten men when Robinson was sent off for a second bookable offence. The Swindon fans were singing, '2-0 and you f——ed it up!', which came without reply from the stunned Argyle fans.

But wait, from the resulting free-kick Luke McCormick launched the ball deep into the Swindon half, Mickey Evans got the flick on and Marino Keith was through, one-on-one with the goalkeeper. He couldn't miss, surely?

He didn't, and the away following simply erupted into jubilant scenes, having seen Argyle score with what turned out to be the last kick of the game. The Argyle fans taunted the home fans with chants of, '2-2, and you f——ed it up!' as the Swindon fans streamed to the exits in disgust.

As we left the stadium, there was a real belief amongst all the fans there that we could achieve something special that season. On the way home, we passed the Exeter supporters' coach and, as a laugh, my mate's dad told us to moon the coach as we passed it. We duly did, and the look on the driver's face was priceless.

Shaun Sandell

I wouldn't go to this game. I told my pals that I had never witnessed a win at the County Ground, so I stayed at home. Much to the annoyance of my pals, as I'm the one with the company car and free petrol!

My away 'system' is always the same. My wife takes the dog out for a walk in Plymbridge with her mate, whilst I listen to Sparksy. It's quite simple – she's a jinx! That day, she came back early because it

Swindon Town 2

Argyle 3

Capaldi, Norris, Keith

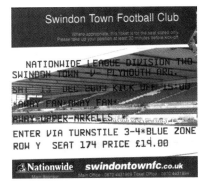

Above left: The team celebrate Marino's last-ditch winner.

Above right: An unbelievable match as Argyle fight back to win 3-2 at the County Ground.

was 'too cold and wet'. Not a problem, thinks I, we're 2-0 up and it looks like my not going to the game has worked.

As she walks through the door – 2-1. 'That's your fault,' says I. 'Don't be so stupid,' says she. Then, unbelievably, 2-2! I could hear their fans singing something like '2-0 and you mucked it up'. I'm livid. 'Right, you, outside', and I pushed my darling wife out through the French window, in that awful weather. I'm not sure who was more shocked, Lyn or the dog.

Suddenly Sparksy bellows something about Marino Keith in the box. Yes! 3-2 to the Champions. My Mrs, outside in the wet, looking at me, a fifty-year-old father of two, jumping about like an idiot. That day, I realised two things:

1) Argyle were going up.

2) My wife is a jinx.

Ian Newell

Like everyone else, I have fond memories of the late drama and the timing of the goal to coincide with the Swindon chanting. However, I also have memories of a panic to get to the match.

On the Friday, I was leaving work in a downpour and, while waiting at Marsh Mills roundabout, there was a horrible grinding noise and my windscreen wiper stopped in the middle of my windscreen. The forecast for the weekend was not too good, and all I could think was, 'I'm going to miss the match tomorrow!'

I got home carefully and then had a mad ring around to get a hire car to be picked up first thing on Saturday morning. Overall, the trip cost me a hire car, windscreen wiper motor and a lot of stress, but the outcome and the manner in which the game was won was well worth it. I also got completely freaked out by the 'magic roundabout'.

Keith Greening

Argyle: McCormick, Connolly, Coughlan, Aljofree, Gilbert, Norris, Wotton, Hodges, Capaldi, Lowndes (Evans), Keith.

ARGYLE v. CHESTERFIELD

Date: 3 January 2004
Location: Home Park

Football League Division Two
Attendance: 13,109

I really wasn't meant to be at this game, as I should have been recovering from a New Year's Eve party hangover in London but, as it was, I was reprieved by a bout of twenty-four hour 'flu. This meant my return to London was delayed, so I decided I would stay for this game after all. I remember thinking that it probably wouldn't be a particularly exciting game. I think it was also after this game that I realised we really were up there with the big guns.

I delayed my whole family's trip to Home Park that day going on about the old days when I didn't leave Elburton until 2.20p.m. and still got a parking space at the edge of Central Park. Alas, as I found out, to my cost (my father shouting very loudly), that sort of behaviour doesn't work anymore and leaving at 2p.m. means you enter parking space hell. Anyway, the rest of us left him to park and legged it into the ground, arriving just in time to see the team come out. As we discovered, this was not a game to miss the start of.

The first twenty minutes passed in a bit of a blur. Friio had one his finest days in a green shirt and I remember feeling happily gobsmacked. I don't think anybody believed it was going to be that easy. The rest of the game was a bit tame in comparison with that first blistering spell, but it was only fitting that Friio should top off such a fine performance with the first Argyle hat-trick since Paul McGregor against Torquay in March 2000. I don't think I stopped grinning for several days following my return to London.

My dad maintains that, because of my lateness, he missed the first goal whilst parking the car. I know, however, that this isn't true because I saw him sneak in to the front of the Lyndhurst just before it went in from my vantage point in the Devonport End! Mind you, he didn't actually get to his seat with the others until after the first twenty minutes!

Laura Naldrett

5-0 in eighteen minutes. OK, the Chesterfield defence was statuesque, helpless, frozen in horror. OK, we were on a run of pretty darn fine form, beating, and expecting to beat, pretty much anyone we came up against.

But even so, this was a historic performance. Have Chelsea ever scored five in the first eighteen? Have Arsenal? Have Manchester United? Have they buggery!

If you've got a DVD player, you'll have seen the goals already. I remember three things above all. I remember turning to whoever it was next to me (block twelve, Lyndhurst) after the third one went in and saying, 'They just can't cope with Phillips out there', and him turning back to me and responding, 'They can't cope with ANY of 'em out there!' He was right, but so was I. Buster had got one of his all-too-rare starts that season and he murdered them down the right-hand side. I also remember the corner for the fourth goal (Friio's first) and saying, while the ball hung in the air, '4-0'. It was that easy.

I remember being so disappointed that, clearly under instructions, the Greens sat back in the second half. Yes, I know we had a long campaign ahead of us. Yes, I know how foolish it would have been to risk

---

Argyle 7
Hodges, Capaldi, Lowndes (2), Friio (3)

Chesterfield 0

David Friio
on the way to
a hat-trick as
Chesterfield
are humbled at
Home Park.

Not a match to be
late for.

injury in such circumstances. Yes, I know Chesterfield, six down, would play for pride in the second half. But I still think we could – and should – have got ten that afternoon. Hell, we weren't far off getting ten in the first half.

That would have been a club record, and, I think, the first ten-goal haul in the English League for the best part of twenty years. Still, it was the first season I can remember there being a six-goal and a seven-goal haul at Home Park – almost as good as the QPR game.

Jim Benton-Evans.

Argyle: McCormick, Connolly, Coughlan, Aljofree, Gilbert, Phillips (Norris), Friio, Hodges, Capaldi (Stonebridge), Lowndes, Evans (Keith).

ARGYLE v. QUEENS PARK RANGERS

Date: 24 April 2004

Location: Home Park

Football League Division Two

Attendance: 19,888

And so it came to this. For weeks this fixture had been looming large on the calendar. All the stresses and strains of the previous months could be wiped away in one afternoon. Defeat the R's and we would be promoted – if Brighton could hold City, then the medal would be ours as well.

During the week leading up to the game, I had been strangely calm, but as we left Richmond early on Saturday morning, the tension started to rise.

After dumping the car at my mother's and taking in the final minutes of the PASALB-PASTA football match around the corner, it was time to head to the Britannia for the first of several pre-match stiffeners. The atmosphere in the pub was electric as we exchanged friendly banter with the R's fans. This was to be a recurring feature of the day – despite the fact that so much rode on the outcome of the game, the camaraderie between the rival sets of supporters was fantastic. The mutual loathing of Luton in the previous championship season had been replaced by a reflected respect for our rivals.

The nervous tension was increasing as kick-off approached. Thousands were milling around in the Central Park sunshine, taking in the atmosphere and even having picnics in the car park. An attempt to get in the Far Post Club was forfeited in favour of a few more cans on the Outland Road verge.

Then, it was time to enter the 'Theatre of Greens'. By now, I was beginning to lose it. I have read of the 'thousand-yard stare' that Vietnam veterans developed after some time 'in country' and I felt myself going the same way. Having met with the friends I was sitting with in the Devonport End, I sought to calm my disposition with more alcohol and even attempted to eat a Various Pie. One mouthful was all I got through. More beer seemed the only answer as I roamed around seeking reassuring noises from old friends like Stuart Caskey, Keef Newham, Andy Mole, Peggy Prior and Andy Laidlaw. All were in a similarly fevered state.

For me, the game was a combination of mental torture and nervous excitement, right until Mickey Evans rose majestically between his markers to head home a David Norris cross in front of the Devonport End.

The collective roar that swept around Home Park must have broken decibel records. The sense of relief and exultation that greeted the goal was truly amazing. The party could start, as it seemed impossible that Rangers could respond to the hammer blow of such a late goal. Then it got better – much better.

Just a few minutes left and a midfield melee a few yards in front of the R's box saw the ball bounce into the path of David Friio. He spun away from the Rangers' defence and danced forward into the box, with only the advancing keeper to beat. 'Chip it!' screamed the Devonport End, and the Gallic maestro duly obliged – a beautiful goal to set the seal on the result.

Pandemonium is not a big enough word to describe the tumultuous response to the second goal. How apt it was that the decisive stroke of the game should come from the player who, perhaps more than any other, epitomised the renaissance of Argyle. When he arrived out of nowhere for the Exeter derby in December 2000, few would have believed how important a player he would become and how the team Paul Sturrock built around him would go on to such heights.

Argyle 2

Evans, Friio

Queens Park Rangers 0

ARGYLE v. QUEENS PARK RANGERS

Above: Trigger scores the first as Argyle are crowned Champions – again.

Right: The bench goes mad as the game concludes.

The final whistle went after three minutes of ball-shielding silliness in the Devonport corner – which nearly provoked Steve Palmer to break Trigger's legs at one point – and then the party could really begin. All the old chestnuts were trotted out on the PA – Queen, Status Quo and Tina Turner. But when the Bristol City result was read out, we all knew that we were Champions, again. The players were popping the champagne and waving the sponsor's flags and the lap of honour went around Home Park twice as the Green Army saluted their heroes.

Eventually, it was time to leave and carry on the celebrations into the night. The stewards were tiring of us as we lingered in the concourse, waiting for *Sky Sports* to scroll the page over to Division Two just one more time. 'You already know the result don't you? What do you need to see it on the telly for?' They

ARGYLE v. QUEENS PARK RANGERS

were ignored and were further irritated when we cheered as the screen told us one more time – 'We Are The Champions!'

We gathered outside Pilgrims Way, mostly in a stupefied daze, not wanting to leave and still coming to terms with the fact that we had witnessed two championships in three years. We strolled our way through Central Park, in search of a celebratory pint at the Pennycomequick. The D&C firmly discouraged this plan as the pub was full of disconsolate QPR fans, so we trundled our way down to the city centre to the Corner House near Frankfort Gate.

A couple of pints later, on we went to the Barbican in time to see the rest of the D&C outside the Noah's Ark, earning their overtime pay by containing twenty or so troublemakers. Twenty out of twenty thousand. Guess which got the most coverage on the TV news that night?

The first port of call for a night on the Barbican is the Notte Inn, where we were greeted with a degree of disdain at first: 'Here they are – all coming out of the woodwork now Argo are winning again'. As soon as we established our credentials (Macclesfield 1-4, Cheltenham 2-5, the Austria tour and so on), apologies were made and a free plate of very hot chips was plonked in front of us. This was the first thing I had eaten in about twelve hours and they went down very well.

On we went into Southside Street, to the alcoholic home of Argyle, the Dolphin. Here we settled in for the duration, taking in the sights and sounds of the Barbican on a warm spring evening. Everywhere you looked, there were Argyle shirts being proudly sported. A lone Manchester United shirt wearer was roundly humiliated as he passed by on his way to the chip shop – how sweet a moment that was.

Eventually, we were joined by some of the board – Paul Stapleton, Robert Dennerly and their partners. A rousing chorus of 'Sack the Board' was aired, with all joining in. A policeman wandered around the corner at this point, to be hailed with an 'On your own, on your own' chant. He smiled nervously and turned away as soon as he could.

We then wandered over to the Three Crowns, where we were joined by Peter Jones and his partner. Ben tried to get him to drink a flaming sambuca, but Peter didn't get where he is today by saying yes to that kind of drink.

We were beginning to fade by now, and a curry was called for. We made our way around the corner to the Ali Ba Ba, near the bus station. Incredibly, they let us in. Given the end-of-meal food fight with mints and orange slices that finished off the night, we may be lucky to get in there again.

The following morning saw us all in a poor state, but we managed to gather ourselves for a McDonald's breakfast (my first and last) before motoring out of Devon while listening to Sparksy's Radio Devon phone-in. We even stopped in a lay-by to hear Paul Stapleton speak before we drifted out of the reception area. Attempts to find a pub serving food along the A303 failed, until we found a wonderful place selling cream teas. It capped a damn fine weekend.

John Lloyd

One of the QPR people had forgotten to buy a programme, so we gave them one of ours and he gave us four cans of beer to say thank you. My brothers wanted to drink them on the train, but Mum said to wait until we got home.

When we got back to Newton Abbot, people were tooting their horns and waving as we walked back to our house, we kept singing 'Championes' and waving back. We could not stop talking about it for ages.

It was really nice that the QPR fans and Argyle fans were friendly. I will always like QPR for being so

The Devonport
End mob the team
(photo courtesy of
Gary Taylor).

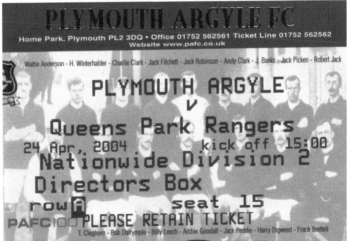

A nerve-shredding finale to the
season.

nice and also for finally getting second place over Bristol City. Even if we get to the Premiership, that day
in April 2004 will always be a very special day for me.

Josh Harvey (aged ten at the time)

Argyle: McCormick, Connolly, Coughlan, Aljofree, Gilbert, Capaldi, Norris, Friio, Hodges, Evans, Keith (Lowndes).

ARGYLE v. IPSWICH TOWN

Date: 30 April 2006
Location: Home Park

Coca Cola Championship
Attendance: 15,921

These are the things that dreams are made of. A living legend scores the winning goal in his last game for his hometown club after more than 400 appearances, stretched over fifteen years.

It just could not have been scripted any better for Mickey Evans to head in the winner for Argyle after coming back from being a goal down.

Tony Pulis had included Evans in the starting line-up after much debate amongst the Argyle fans in the build-up to the game. There was a carnival atmosphere around the ground with the end-of-term feel highlighted by the sale of jester hats outside of the ground.

In an early attack, Akos Buzsaky, playing wide on the right, set up David Norris but he shot over from twelve yards out. Romain Larrieu then pulled off a fine save to deny Ipswich at the expense of a corner.

Then disaster, and proof that Ipswich didn't read the script for the 'Evans' game. A long, curling cross from the by-line was missed by Larrieu and the Ipswich striker Nicky Forster out-jumped Paul Connolly to head in. 1-0 to Ipswich.

Argyle huffed and puffed and finally got back into the game, with Michael Evans involved in the goal. A Paul Wotton long ball was headed across goal by Evans and Tony Capaldi and Vincent Pericard were unmarked in the area. Both of them got into a mix-up over who should thump the ball into the net, but after what seemed like an age and some disco dancing from both players, Capaldi finally took the responsibility and thumped the ball in. 1-1.

Then Evans was involved again when he unleashed a tremendous left-foot shot that was destined to go in, but the Ipswich keeper somehow managed to tip the ball away for a corner.

Argyle piled on the pressure early in the second half with Capaldi and Evans prominent in all things good about Argyle. And then came that moment.

A Capaldi free-kick into the area was flicked on by Pericard and up popped Evans with a diving header to send the ball into the far corner. Chaos then broke out as every Argyle player, including Larrieu, jumped on top of Evans who was on the bottom of a mass green-shirted orgy. The noise from the stands was deafening.

After what seemed like an age, Mickey emerged from the body pile and took the acclaim of the fans. Pure fantasy. The game and atmosphere now went up a notch.

Capaldi had a header saved and then Buzsaky sent Mickey clean through on goal with only the keeper to beat. But the Ipswich keeper spoilt the party and made a great save to deny Trigger.

The stadium erupted for the second time when Evans was substituted for Nick Chadwick and got a tremendous standing ovation, even from the Ipswich fans. Larrieu made his second trip of the day past the halfway line as every Argyle player shook hands with Trigger. Off walked a true Argyle legend.

Argyle 2
  Capaldi, Evans

Ipswich Town 1

Above left: Trigger signs off in style with the winner.

Above right: An emotional farewell for the hometown striker.

It was the typical Evans performance. Barging around, linking up play, winning free-kicks, but this time he popped up with a goal. His name was chanted throughout the second half.

Ian De-Lar

In a season that had been a little light on memorable moments, the finale was full of them. We had learnt, in the days leading up to the game, that Mickey Evans was to leave Home Park after this game, his 432nd in a green shirt and it put another 2,000 on the gate. The Green Army came to pay tribute to their local hero and he did not let them down.

His career at Argyle perhaps did not feature enough goals, but when he did score, it was often at a vital moment. Who could forget his goal in the play-off semi-final against Colchester in 1996? Or the two he bagged against York when we had forgotten how to win outside Devon for over a year in 2001? Or the cheeky free-kick off the Swindon keeper in 2004? The header against QPR is seared on the memory of us all and here and, as he faced his final curtain, he did it again – a diving header in front of the Devonport End to win the game from 1-0 down. Roy of the Rovers stuff. A fairytale ending for one of Argyle's finest servants – the only Pilgrim to win promotion three times.

John Lloyd

Argyle: Larrieu, Connolly, Wotton, Aljofree, Hodges, Buzsaky (Pulis), Norris, Nalis, Capaldi, Pericard (Reid), Evans (Chadwick).

Other titles published by STADIA

Voices of Home Park
JOHN LLOYD

These are the stories and memories of fans who have followed Argyle through thick and thin down the year, through promotions and relegations, epic cup runs and crushing defeats, the strange and sometimes hilarious events that have marked Argyle's 100 years as a professional club.

0 7524 2949 3

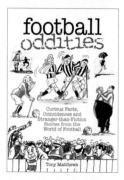

Football Oddities
TONY MATTHEWS

In one of the most individual and irreverent collections of footballing facts ever produced, Tony Matthews has unearthed tales of the unexpected that will delight footy fans everywhere. Did you hear the one about the Argentine full-back who scored a hat-trick of own goals in less than an hour? Remember the England goalkeeper who was sent off after just twenty-seven seconds of a Premiership game in 1995? Read about them – and many, many others – here.

0 7524 3401 8

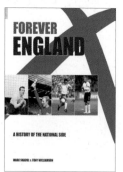

Forever England A History of the National Side
MARK SHAOUL & TONY WILLIAMSON

From the days of the amateur gentlemen of the 1870s to the present day, *Forever England* is an insightful and fascinating account of the history of the country's national football team. England's finest hour in 1966 is covered in detail, as are the other highs and lows of 130 years of international competition. This enthralling narrative, which includes England team line-ups for key games, match reports and group tables from all major tournaments, is richly illustrated with over 200 images.

0 7524 2939 7

Plymouth Speedway
PAUL EUSTACE

The Plymouth Speedway team raced at Pennycross for twenty-two seasons between 1931 and 1970. Now, at the beginning of a new era for Plymouth Speedway, this book enables the people of the South West to look back at the team's earlier years; the good and bad times; the great riders and classic meetings. Featuring over 200 illustrations, this book will delight not only Plymouth fans but anyone who remembers the golden years of British speedway.

0 7524 4023 3

If you are interested in purchasing other books published by Stadia, or in case you have difficulty finding any Stadia books in your local bookshop, you can also place orders directly through the Tempus Publishing website
www.tempus-publishing.com